The Conference
on Antarctica

Washington

October 15–December 1, 1959

Conference Documents
The Antarctic Treaty
and Related Papers

HEAD OF UNITED STATES DELEGATION SIGNING THE ANTARCTIC TREATY. Amb
sador Herman Phleger is shown signing the Antarctic Treaty on December
1959. Ambassador Paul C. Daniels, Alternate United States Representati
(standing), is looking on. Secretary of State Christian A. Herter is seated l
hind Ambassador Phleger.

Foreword

This volume contains public documents of the Conference on Antarctica, held at Washington from October 15 to December 1, 1959, which resulted in the signing of the Antarctic Treaty. It includes the text of the Treaty and various related papers. All the papers have previously been released.

Contents

Heads of the Delegations to the Conference on Antarctica in Washington
Standing, left to right: Marcial Mora (*Chile*), Viscount Obert de Thieusies (*Belgium*), G. D. L. White (*New Zealand*), Viscount Hood (*United Kingdom*), Paul Koht (*Norway*), W. C. du Plessis (*Union of South Africa*), Henry Allen (*Secretary General of the Conference*), and Takeso Shimoda (*Japan*). Seated, left to right: Howard Beale (*Australia*), Adolfo Scilingo (*Argentina*), Chairman of the Conference Herman Phleger (*United States*), Grigory I. Tunkin (*Soviet Union*), Pierre Charpentier (*France*). Photograph of November 1959.

List of Participants [1]

Officers of the Conference

Chairman

Herman Phleger, Ambassador (*United States*)

Secretary General

Henry E. Allen, Office of International Conferences, Department of State

United States Delegation

Representative

Head of Delegation

Herman Phleger, Ambassador

Alternate Representatives

Paul C. Daniels, Ambassador; Special Adviser on Antarctica, Department of State

George H. Owen, Director, Antarctica Staff, Department of State

Congressional Advisers

Frank Carlson, Member, Foreign Relations Committee, United States Senate
Gale W. McGee, Member, Interstate and Foreign Commerce Committee, United States Senate

Advisers

Captain Eugene W. Davis, USN, Department of Defense
Larkin H. Farinholt, Office of the Science Adviser, Department of State
Alton W. Hemba, Bureau of Inter-American Affairs, Department of State
Milan W. Jerabek, Bureau of European Affairs, Department of State
Alan F. Neidle, Office of the Legal Adviser, Department of State
Henry C. Reed, Bureau of Inter-American Affairs, Department of State
Arthur H. Rosen, Bureau of Far Eastern Affairs, Department of State
Robert M. Schneider, Bureau of African Affairs, Department of State

Secretary of Delegation

Wayne W. Fisher, Antarctica Staff, Department of State

Argentine Delegation

Representative

Head of Delegation

Adolfo Scilingo, Ambassador; Special Adviser to the President

---

[1] Based on Conf. doc. 3 (Rev. 1), Nov. 17, 1959.

---

*Present only through Nov. 6.

Representatives—Continued

Enrique Gajardo, Ambassador; Legal Adviser to the National Antarctic Commission, Ministry of Foreign Affairs

Julio Escudero, Ambassador; Professor of International Law, University of Chile

Alternate Representative

Horacio Suárez, Minister, Embassy at Washington

Advisers

Manuel Bianchi, Counselor, Embassy at Washington
Colonel Otto Barth, Military Attaché, Embassy at Washington
Captain Jorge Swett, Naval Attaché, Embassy at Washington
Colonel Rogelio Gonzalez, Air Attaché, Embassy at Washington
Oscar Pinochet, First Secretary, Embassy at Buenos Aires

Secretary of Delegation

Carlos Reyes, Chief of Information, Chilean Nitrate Sales Corporation, Santiago

French Delegation

Representative

Head of Delegation

Pierre Charpentier, Ambassador

Alternate Representative

Guy Scalabre, Counselor of Embassy, Ministry of Foreign Affairs

Principal Adviser

André Gros, Legal Adviser, Ministry of Foreign Affairs

Advisers

Claude Chayet, Counselor of Embassy, Legal Adviser to the French Delegation to the United Nations

Commander Yves Delrieu, Assistant Naval Attaché, Embassy at Washington

Secretary of Delegation

Jacques Andreani, Second Secretary, Embassy at Washington

Japanese Delegation

Representatives

Head of Delegation

Koichiro Asakai, Ambassador to the United States

Takeso Shimoda, Minister, Embassy at Washington

Advisers

Masahiro Nishibori, First Secretary, Embassy at Washington
Hiroshi Nemoto, Chief, International Conventions Section, Treaty Bureau, Ministry of Foreign Affairs
Shinyichi Sugihara, First Secretary, Embassy at Washington
Kimiro Fujita, Attaché, Embassy at Washington

New Zealand Delegation

Representatives

Head of Delegation

*Walter Nash, Prime Minister and Minister of External Affairs

Deputy Head of Delegation

A. D. McIntosh, Secretary of External Affairs

Alternate Representative

G. D. L. White, Chargé d'Affaires ad interim at Washington

Advisers

R. M. Miller, First Secretary, Embassy at Washington

R. L. Jermyn, Department of External Affairs

D. G. Harper, Third Secretary, Embassy at Washington

F. A. Small, Legal Division, Department of External Affairs

Norwegian Delegation

Representatives

Head of Delegation

Paul Koht, Ambassador to the United States

Deputy Head of Delegation

Torfinn Oftedal, Counselor, Embassy at Washington

Alternate Representatives

Rear Admiral Dagfinn E. Kjeholt, Naval Attaché, Embassy at Washington
Commander Oddmund P. Aakenes, Assistant Naval Attaché, Embassy at Washington

Dr. Anders K. Orvin, Director, Norwegian Polar Institute, Oslo

Gunnar Haerum, First Secretary, Ministry of Foreign Affairs

Secretary of Delegation

Nils Vogt, Second Secretary, Embassy at Washington

Union of South Africa Delegation

Representatives

Head of Delegation

†Eric H. Louw, Minister of External Affairs

Deputy Head of Delegation

W. C. du Plessis, Ambassador to the United States

Alternate Representatives

J. G. Stewart, Counselor, Embassy at Washington

A. G. Dunn, First Secretary, Embassy at Washington

D. Stuart Franklin, Second Secretary, Embassy at Washington

---

* Arrived in Washington on Oct. 25 and attended Conference meetings from Oct. 27 through 29, the day of his departure.

†Attended only the first two plenary sessions of the Conference, on Oct. 15 and 16.

Advisers

Dr. R. G. Shuttleworth, Scientific Attaché, Embassy at Washington
Louis Vorster, Third Secretary, Embassy at Washington

Soviet Delegation

Representatives

Head of Delegation

Vasili V. Kuznetsov, First Deputy Minister for Foreign Affairs

Grigory I. Tunkin, Head of the Treaty and Legal Department, Ministry for Foreign Affairs

Alternate Representatives

Alexander A. Afanasiev, Head of the Main Administration of the Northern Sea Route, Ministry of Merchant Marine
Vice Admiral Valentin A. Chekurov, Head, Navy Hydrographic Service
Mikhail M. Somov, Deputy Director, Institute of Arctic and Antarctic Scientific Research, Ministry of Merchant Marine, Leningrad
Mikhail N. Smirnovsky, Counselor, Embassy at Washington

Advisers

Yuri V. Filippov, Counselor, Embassy at Washington
Alexander M. Gusev, Deputy Director, Institute of Applied Geophysics, Academy of Science of the U.S.S.R.
Jousuf K. Djavad, Deputy Chief, Department for Foreign Relations, Ministry of Merchant Marine
Stepan V. Molodtsov, Senior Scientific Research Staff Member, Institute of Law, Academy of Science of the U.S.S.R.
Anatoly P. Movchan, Second Secretary, Treaty and Legal Department, Ministry for Foreign Affairs; Secretary of Delegation
Gennady S. Stashevsky, Third Secretary, Department of the International Organizations, Ministry for Foreign Affairs

United Kingdom Delegation

Representatives

Head of Delegation

*Sir Esler Dening

†Sir Harold Caccia, Ambassador to the United States

Alternate Representatives

H. N. Brain, Assistant Under-Secretary of State, Foreign Office
‡Viscount Hood, Minister, Embassy at Washington
H. A. A. Hankey, Head of American Department, Foreign Office

Principal Adviser

Sir Gerald Fitzmaurice, Senior Legal Adviser, Foreign Office

---

*Attended Conference meetings from Oct. 15 through Nov. 19.
†Acted as Representative only at the fourth plenary session of the Conference on Dec. 1.
‡Acted as Representative at Conference meetings from Nov. 20 through 30.

Advisers

Dr. B. B. Roberts, Foreign Office

M. A. Willis, Colonial Office

J. R. Freeland, Foreign Office

D. L. Benest, First Secretary, Embassy at Washington

R. E. C. F. Parsons, Foreign Office, Secretary of Delegation

Principal Members of the International Secretariat

Secretary General

Henry E. Allen, Office of International Conferences, Department of State

Deputy to the Secretary General

Harry V. Ryder, Jr.

Chief, Technical Secretariat Services

Harry W. Shlaudeman

Technical Secretaries

Curtis C. Cutter

Richard A. Dwyer

Thomas H. Englesby

John E. Jackson

Warren H. Reynolds

Treaty Adviser

Eleanor C. McDowell

Public Information Officer

Francis W. Herron

Administrative Officer

Frank England

Security Officer

Leo E. Crampsey

Documents Officer

Bennie Mae Stevens

Deputy Documents Officer

George R. Koontz

Language Services Officer

Edmund S. Glenn

Table of Meetings[1]

(1776 Pennsylvania Avenue, Washington, D.C.) [2]

Type of Meeting	Date	Time
1st plenary session (open to the public)	October 15	11:00 a.m.–12:30 p.m., 3:00–4:30 p.m.
2d plenary session	October 16	10:30 a.m.–12:05 p.m.
Committee I: 1st meeting	October 16	3:00–4:50 p.m.
3d plenary session	October 16	4:50–5:00 p.m.
Committee I: 2d meeting	October 19	10:30 a.m.–12:15 p.m.
Committee II: 1st meeting	October 19	3:00–5:35 p.m.
Committee I: 3d meeting	October 20	10:30–11:58 a.m.
Committee II: 2d meeting	October 20	3:15–5:35 p.m.
Committee I: 4th meeting	October 21	11:00 a.m.
Committee II: 3d meeting	October 21	3:10–5:15 p.m.
Committee I: 5th meeting	October 22	11:00 a.m.
Committee II: 4th meeting	October 22	3:10–5:30 p.m.
Committee I: 6th meeting	October 23	11:00 a.m.

[1] The chief representatives of the various nations at one or more of the meetings were the following: Argentina—Scilingo and Bello; Australia—Casey, Beale, and Booker; Belgium—de Thieusies and van der Essen; Chile—Mora, Gajardo, and Escudero; France—Charpentier and Scalabre; Japan—Asakai, Shimoda, and Nishibori; New Zealand—Nash, McIntosh, White, Miller, and Jermyn; Norway—Koht and Oftedal; South Africa—Louw, du Plessis, and Stewart; Soviet Union—Kuznetsov, Tunkin, and Afanasiev; United Kingdom—Dening, Brain, Caccia, and Hood; United States—Phleger, Daniels, and Owen.

[2] The opening plenary session was held at the Department of the Interior Auditorium.

Type of Meeting	Date	Time
Committee II: 5th meeting	October 23	3:10–5:45 p.m.
Committee I: 7th meeting	October 26	11:00 a.m.–12:33 p.m.
Committee II: 6th meeting	October 26	3:10–5:30 p.m.
Committee I: 8th meeting	October 27	11:00 a.m.–12:30 p.m.
Committee II: 7th meeting	October 27	3:10–5:50 p.m.
Committee I: 9th meeting	October 28	11:00 a.m.–12:48 p.m.
Committee II: 8th meeting	October 28	3:10–5:45 p.m.
Committee I: 10th meeting	October 29	11:00 a.m.–12:35 p.m.
Committee II: 9th meeting	October 29	3:07–5:35 p.m.
Committee I: 11th meeting	October 30	11:00 a.m.–12:38 p.m.
Heads of Delegation meeting[1]	October 30	3:00 p.m.
Heads of Delegation meeting	November 2	p.m.
Committee of the Whole: 1st meeting	November 3	11:10 a.m.–12:30 p. m.
Committee of the Whole: 2d meeting	November 3	3:15–5:27 p.m.
Heads of Delegation meeting	November 4	ended at 12:48 p.m.
Committee of the Whole: 3d meeting	November 4	3:15–4:15 p.m.
Heads of Delegation meeting	November 4	4:40 p.m.
Heads of Delegation meeting	November 5	a.m.
Heads of Delegation meeting	November 5	p.m.
Heads of Delegation meeting	November 6	a.m.
Heads of Delegation meeting	November 6	p.m.
Committee of the Whole: 4th meeting	November 6	5:16–5:35 p.m.
Heads of Delegation meeting	November 9	a.m.
Heads of Delegation meeting	November 9	p.m.

[1] The Heads of Delegation meetings were informal. By mutual agreement participation was usually limited to the Heads of Delegation or designated representatives. The morning and afternoon meetings of the Heads of Delegation were normally scheduled to begin at 10:30 a.m. and 3:00 p.m.

Type of Meeting	Date	Time
Committee of the Whole: 5th meeting	November 9	5:15–5:50 p.m.
Heads of Delegation meeting	November 10	a.m.
Heads of Delegation meeting	November 10	p.m.
Heads of Delegation meeting	November 11	a.m.
Heads of Delegation meeting	November 11	p.m.
Heads of Delegation meeting	November 12	a.m.
Committee of the Whole: 6th meeting	November 12	3:15–4:13 p.m.
Heads of Delegation meeting	November 13	p.m.
Heads of Delegation meeting	November 16	a.m.
Heads of Delegation meeting	November 17	9:30 a.m.–12:30 p.m.
Heads of Delegation meeting	November 17	3:00 p.m.
Heads of Delegation meeting	November 18	10:30 a. m.
Heads of Delegation meeting	November 19	10:30 a.m.
Heads of Delegation meeting	November 20	a.m.
Heads of Delegation meeting	November 20	3:15 p.m.
Heads of Delegation meeting	November 23	10:00 a.m.
Heads of Delegation meeting	November 24	10:30 a.m.
Heads of Delegation meeting	November 25	10:30 a.m.
Heads of Delegation meeting	November 27	10:30 a.m.
Heads of Delegation meeting	November 28	10:30 a.m.
Committee of the Whole: 7th meeting	November 30	2:40 –5:35 p.m.
4th plenary session (open to the press)	December 1	10:00–11:43 a.m.

Opening Plenary Session, October 15

MORNING MEETING (11:00 a.m.–12:30 p.m.)

Secretary of State Christian A. Herter, Presiding

Conf. doc. 4, October 15, 1959

Welcoming Statement by Secretary of State Herter

It is a pleasure and an honor for me, on behalf of the Government of the United States, to welcome to Washington the distinguished representatives and advisers who compose the delegations to the Conference on Antarctica.

We are meeting here for the purpose of reaching an agreement concerning a vast continent. Long a mystery, later the scene of heroic adventure and exploration, this continent is now an area of the world in which international scientific cooperation, for the benefit of mankind, has been successfully demonstrated to an outstanding degree by the brave men of the nations here represented who participated in the Antarctic programs of the International Geophysical Year.

My Government is dedicated to the principle that the continuation of this cooperation should be assured, and that Antarctica should be used for peaceful purposes only, should not become an object of political conflict, and should be open for the conduct of scientific investigations.

The exertions of the explorers and scientists of nations represented here have made possible this opportunity to formulate and give legal effect to certain high principles which, in consonance with the Charter of the United Nations, would ensure peace and cooperation in a vast area of the world. The Conference will undertake this task with confidence.

The United States, as host country, welcomes you. We wish you a pleasant stay here and look forward to a successful conference.

[EDITORIAL NOTE: At this point Mr. Phleger was elected Permanent Chairman of the Conference and Henry E. Allen was appointed Secretary General. Mr. Herter relinquished the chair to Mr. Phleger.]

1

Statement by Mr. Phleger (*United States*)

Governor Herter has other pressing engagements and must now leave. Thank you, Secretary Herter, for your words of welcome and your good wishes for the success of our deliberations. Will Ambassador Daniels please take the seat of Representative of the United States of America.

First, may I express my appreciation of the high honor which you have conferred upon me in electing me Chairman of this International Conference on Antarctica. I realize, of course, that my selection is as a representative of the United States of America, and that the honor is one bestowed upon my country, the host country, an honor which is deeply appreciated.

This is indeed a unique and important conference convened as it is to deal with the vital subjects of the pursuit of peace and international cooperation in the field of scientific research. There is added challenge in that the subject of our deliberations is the vast continent of Antarctica. I know our efforts will draw inspiration from the example of the heroic explorers and scientists who dedicated their lives to the discovery of the secrets of this great continent.

At this time it would seem appropriate to read the invitation issued in connection with the convening of this conference. On May 3 [2] 1958, Ambassadors of the United States delivered to each of the governments represented here, identical notes reading as follows:

EXCELLENCY: I have the honor to refer to the splendid example of international cooperation which can now be observed in many parts of the world because of the coordinated efforts of scientists of many countries in seeking a better understanding of geophysical phenomena during the current International Geophysical Year. These coordinated efforts of the scientists of many lands have as their objective a greatly increased knowledge of the planet on which we live and will no doubt contribute directly and indirectly to the welfare of the human race for many generations to come

Among the various portions of the globe where these cooperative scientific endeavors are being carried on with singular success and with a sincere consciousness of the high ideals of mankind to which they are dedicated is the vast and relatively remote continent of Antarctica. The scientific research being conducted in that continent by the cooperative efforts of distinguished scientists from many countries is producing information of practical as well as theoretical value for all mankind.

The International Geophysical Year comes to a close at the end of 1958 The need for coordinated scientific research in Antarctica, however, will continue for many more years into the future. Accordingly, it would appear desirable for those countries participating in the Antarctic program of the International Geophysical Year to reach agreement among themselves on a program to assure the continuation of the fruitful scientific cooperation referred to above. Such an arrangement could have the additional ad

2

vantage of preventing unnecessary and undesirable political rivalries in that continent, the uneconomic expenditure of funds to defend individual national interests, and the recurrent possibility of international misunderstanding. It would appear that if harmonious agreement can be reached among the countries directly concerned in regard to friendly cooperation in Antarctica, there would be advantages not only to those countries but to all other countries as well.

The present situation in Antarctica is characterized by diverse legal, political, and administrative concepts which render friendly cooperation difficult in the absence of an understanding among the countries involved. Seven countries have asserted claims of sovereignty to portions of Antarctica, some of which overlap and give rise to occasional frictions. Other countries have a direct interest in that continent based on past discovery and exploration, geographic proximity, sea and air transportation routes, and other considerations.

The United States for many years has had, and at the present time continues to have, direct and substantial rights and interests in Antarctica. Throughout a period of many years, commencing in the early eighteen-hundreds, many areas of the Antarctic region have been discovered, sighted, explored and claimed on behalf of the United States by nationals of the United States and by expeditions carrying the flag of the United States. During this period, the Government of the United States and its nationals have engaged in well-known and extensive activities in Antarctica.

In view of the activities of the United States and its nationals referred to above, my Government reserves all of the rights of the United States with respect to the Antarctic region, including the right to assert a territorial claim or claims.

It is the opinion of my Government, however, that the interests of mankind would best be served, in consonance with the high ideals of the Charter of the United Nations, if the countries which have a direct interest in Antarctica were to join together in the conclusion of a treaty which would have the following peaceful purposes :

A. Freedom of scientific investigation throughout Antarctica by citizens, organizations, and governments of all countries; and a continuation of the international scientific cooperation which is being carried out so successfully during the current International Geophysical Year.

B. International agreement to ensure that Antarctica be used for peaceful purposes only.

C. Any other peaceful purposes not inconsistent with the Charter of the United Nations.

The Government of the United States is prepared to discuss jointly with the Governments of the other countries having a direct interest in Antarctica the possibility of concluding an agreement, which would be in the form of a treaty, for the purpose of giving legal effect to these high principles. It is believed that such a treaty can be concluded without requiring any participating nation to renounce whatever basic historic rights it may have in Antarctica, or whatever claims of sovereignty it may have asserted. It could be specifically provided that such basic rights and such claims would remain unaffected while the treaty is in force, and that no new rights would be acquired and no new claims made by any country during the duration of the treaty. In other words, the legal status quo in Antarctica would be frozen for the duration of the treaty, permitting cooperation in scientific and administrative matters to be carried out in a constructive manner without being hampered or affected in any way by political considerations. Provision could likewise be made for such joint administrative arrangements as might be necessary and desirable to ensure the successful accomplishment of the agreed objectives. The proposed treaty would be deposited with the United Nations, and the cooperation of the specialized technical agencies of the United Nations would be sought. Such an arrangement would provide a firm and favorable foundation for a continuation of the productive activities which have thus far distinguished the International Geophysical Year; would provide an agreed basis for the maintenance of peaceful and orderly conditions in Antarctica during years to come; and would avoid the possibility of that continent becoming the scene of international discord.

In the hope that the countries having a direct interest in Antarctica will agree on the desirability of the aforesaid high objectives, and will work together in an effort to convert them into practical realities, the Government of the United States has the honor to invite the Government of _____ to participate in a Conference for this purpose to be convened at an early date at such place as may be mutually agreeable.

Accept, Excellency, the renewed assurances of my highest consideration.

This is the time and place agreed upon by the participating governments for the convening of the conference.

Conf. doc. 5, October 15, 1959

Statement by Mr. Louw (*Union of South Africa*)

Mr. Chairman, may I convey to you, on my own behalf, and also on behalf of the members of my delegation, our sincere congratulations on your unanimous election as Chairman of this Conference. Your eminence as a jurist; your wide experience in international affairs; your ability and your wisdom are well known. It is a matter of satisfaction to know that in seeking their common objective the delegates attending this Conference will have the benefit of your wise guidance.

I would also wish to thank the Honourable the Secretary of State, Mr. Herter, for the welcome which he has extended to us. I personally am glad to have the opportunity of being once more in this beautiful city, where I had the honour to be my country's first diplomatic representative from 1929–1933.

Mr. Chairman, my Government is deeply appreciative of the initiative which the United States Government has taken in calling this Conference, and in providing the necessary facilities for holding it in Washington.

The Government of the Union of South Africa has long felt the need for an international cooperative approach to the "question-mark" of Antarctica, in order that this continent may be divorced from the

4

discord and national rivalries which so often have bedevilled coopera-tion among nations in other parts of the world. We therefore wel-comed the proposal of the United States Government, that a Con-ference be held which could draw up a multilateral Treaty, embodying two fundamental principles, viz., that Antarctica shall be used for peaceful purposes only, and secondly that there shall be freedom of, and international cooperation in, scientific investigation in Antarctica.

I am sure that I am voicing the sentiments of all present when I express appreciation of the excellent work that has been done by the representatives of the Governments concerned, during the preliminary discussions. These discussions have helped to clarify our thoughts as to the form of the proposed treaty and prepared the way for con-sideration of the various problems with which we are faced.

The twelve nations represented at this Conference all have a special interest in the Antarctic area. These nations comprise Great Powers and smaller Powers; countries in the Northern, as well as in the South-ern Hemisphere. Their interests are based on a variety of considera-tions, such as discovery, exploration, scientific activity and geo-graphical situation. It is gratifying, and also encouraging that they have been willing to get together in order to seek agreement and also coordination of their activities, and of their respective policies, and above all, that they have agreed that the basis of our approach to this matter should be adherence to the principles of peaceful use, and the freedom of scientific investigation, on an international cooperative basis. These two principles my delegation regards as fundamental to any multilateral agreement in regard to Antarctica. Indeed these principles are mutually dependent and complementary. The South African delegation attaches as much importance to the one, as to the other.

By virtue of South Africa's geographical situation at the Southern end of Africa, and thus the nearest part of that continent to Antarc-tica, it stands to reason that we in South Africa regard events and de-velopments in the Antarctic continent—our Southern neighbour—as of particular importance and of direct and special concern to us.

The strategic importance of Antarctica has become increasingly evident during recent years. Today South Africa is only a few hours flying time away from the Antarctic Continent. The main, and in fact the only sure sea route between the West and the East is around the Cape of Good Hope. Thus, not only for South Africa, but also for all peace-loving nations, it is imperative that this sea route should remain open to the shipping of all nations.

Mr. Chairman, in the discussions which lie ahead, it will be the purpose of my delegation, in cooperation with other delegations, to seek mutually acceptable means of ensuring that the principle of the peaceful use of Antarctica is assured. "Peaceful use" means non-military use, and it should be our aim to ensure non-militarisation of the Antarctic area to the fullest extent possible, consistent with the objectives of the Treaty.

It is only on the basis of an international agreement that Antarctica will not be used for military purposes, and that it will not be the scene of political and international rivalries, that it will be possible to secure international cooperation in scientific investigation and research in that area.

It is a reassuring fact that since the discovery of Antarctica its slow but steady penetration by a number of countries has been characterized by very little friction or dispute. The emphasis has been more on cooperative effort than on political rivalry.

No doubt, that cooperation was made easier by the difficulties and hardships inseparable from the exploration of an unknown and barren area of the world. What is important, however, is that we *have* this basis upon which cooperative effort can be built. This basis for future cooperation was greatly strengthened by the joint activities of the recently concluded International Geophysical Year, in which the twelve countries here represented, participated.

It will readily be agreed that the tempo of scientific and geographic progress was given a tremendous impetus by the International Geophysical Year. There is little doubt that the international cooperation which characterized the International Geophysical Year, largely contributed towards solving some of the scientific problems which have exercised men's minds since time immemorial. Many problems still remain to be solved, and the solution of some may be found in Antarctica. It is our earnest hope that by the cooperative effort of the nations here represented, the success of this undertaking will be assured.

South Africa is eager to play its part in scientific investigation and research in Antarctica. Our scientists have, even in the distant past, shown a keen interest in the Continent, and although we may not have achieved spectacular results, I think I can claim that the records of international cooperation in the scientific investigation of Antarctica will show that the part played by South Africa has not been insignificant.

Because of its geographical position in relation to Antarctica, Cape Town was an important port of call for the early Antarctic explorers of the Nineteenth Century. In the early years of this century South African commercial enterprise turned its attention to the rich harvest which the Antarctic seas offered in whales and seals, and many South African vessels ventured into the dangerous waters of Antarctica and the contiguous islands.

6

Not only did the South African Government contribute to the funds of the Scott Expedition of 1910, but the South African public, whose imagination was stirred by the explorations then taking place, responded generously to an appeal for funds for the expedition. It was in fact at Cape Town that Captain Scott boarded the "Terra Nova" on his last voyage to Antarctica.

A deeper and more extensive scientific knowledge of Antarctica is of the greatest concern to South Africa, not only for the solution of the more important scientific problems of the Southern Hemisphere and in the furtherance of pure research, but also for the purpose of increasing our knowledge and understanding of the natural phenomena of South Africa in various fields—for example, geology, geomagnetism, meteorology, climatology and oceanography. There are geophysical problems which occur in the everyday life of our country, the solution of which, it is believed, will be substantially helped by the results of scientific investigations in Antarctica. It is there, for instance, that our climate is largely fashioned.

Immediately after the first World War the South African Association for the Advancement of Science, in cooperation with our Universities and other scientific institutions, organised a South African Expedition to that part of Antarctica which lies due south of South Africa. It was planned that the Expedition—consisting of about 65 men divided into five parties—would remain on the mainland for three years, in order to undertake geographical and biological research on the mainland, and also in the surrounding seas, particular attention being paid to meteorology and oceanography. Planning for the Expedition had reached an advanced stage, when unfortunately the impact of the first post-war depression prevented its being carried out.

South African interest in Antarctica did not however wane. In 1921 the South African Government nominated Professor Goddard of Stellenbosch University, who had been the prime mover behind the proposed Expedition, to serve on the Overseas Committee for the Shackleton-Rowett Expedition. The South African Government also became an early contributor to the funds of the Scott Polar Research Institute. In 1925, in his presidential address to the British Association for the Advancement of Science, General Smuts made a plea for a coordinated programme of meteorological observation through the establishment by the nations of the Southern Hemisphere of weather stations on Antarctica. Later, in the nineteen thirties, South African scientists participated in the programme of the International Polar Year.[1]

---

[1] This international effort was also called the Second Polar Year (1932–33) in commemoration of the Jubilee of the First International Polar Year (1882–83).

A South African geologist, Dr. A. L. du Toit, took a prominent part in the establishment of the principles of the Continental Drift. In particular, his comparison of the geologies of South America and South Africa led to the general acceptance of the theory of the former contiguity of these continents. According to the same theory, the lands which formerly lay east of South Africa now constitute the eastern side of the Weddell Sea in Antarctica. Rock formations that occur in South Africa occur also in Antarctica.

It was therefore not surprising that the Geological Society of South Africa should take the initiative in 1944 in the formation of a South African Antarctic Research Committee to consider the possibility of a South African Expedition to the Antarctic after the Second World War. The Committee worked actively for a number of years, but again the plans could not be realised.

The fact that imaginative and ambitious plans for independent South African Expeditions to Antarctica could not be realised, illustrates the difficulties facing small countries that wish to undertake a complicated and costly enterprise. Indeed, it was because of these difficulties that South Africa's manifestation of interest in Antarctic research has in the past taken the form of the contribution of men and money to the undertakings of other countries. Thus our participation in the Antarctic programme of the International Geophysical Year was confined to weather observations at Marion, Tristan da Cunha and Gough, and also to contributions to the Commonwealth Trans-Antarctic Expedition.[1] South African meteorologists also were seconded to the British base at Halley Bay; and our Weather Bureau has produced a voluminous and authoritative work entitled "The Meteorology of Antarctica" which has been well received in scientific circles.[2] Furthermore the World Meteorological Office has commissioned the compilation of three weather maps of the world, and the map for that part of the world which is south of the equatorial belt has been entrusted to South Africa's meteorologists.

Against this background it gives me great pleasure now to inform the Conference that the South African Government has recently decided to send a purely South African Scientific Expedition to the mainland of Antarctica. Barring unforeseen circumstances the Expedition will sail from Cape Town next month and will remain on the mainland during the Antarctic winter of 1960. It will be under the leadership of Mr. Hannes Le Grange who was a member of Sir Vivian Fuchs' Commonwealth Trans-Antarctic Expedition. There will be ap-

---

[1] This expedition took place in the years 1955–58.

[2] *Meteorology of the Antarctic*, edited by M. P. van Rooy (Pretoria: Weather Bureau, Department of Transport, 1957).

proximately ten men in the party leaving this year, but it is our hope that we shall, within the limits of our resources of manpower and funds, be able to increase this number in future years. In the preparation for this Expedition we have had the willing cooperation of the Norwegian government and we are negotiating with them for the use of their buildings in Queen Maud Land. A long-term programme of scientific work is being drawn up in consultation with our scientists, and we are confident that the Expedition will make an effective and valuable contribution to the scientific investigation of Antarctica. We are also continuing our activities in the contiguous islands, and hope also to undertake in due course another reconnaissance of Bouvet Island, with a view to investigating the prospects of establishing a weather station there. With this network of island weather stations, together with the station on Antarctica itself, we shall be in a position to make an even more valuable contribution than in the past to the meteorology of these parts.

The South African Government looks forward with confidence to continuing to play its part in the investigation of the scientific phenomena of Antarctica, and sincerely hopes that the fruitful cooperation of past years between the nations represented at this Conference will continue in the future under the shelter of the Treaty for the negotiation of which we are now meeting at Washington. Constructive and cooperative endeavour will, we believe, contribute substantially towards men's conquest of the unknown, and also towards ensuring that Antarctica is used only for peaceful purposes.

On behalf of the South African Government I wish to express the sincere hope that the proceedings of this Conference will successfully terminate in the conclusion of a Treaty which will enshrine the two fundamental principles to which all the Governments represented here subscribe—that Antarctica shall be used for peaceful purposes only and that there shall be freedom of scientific investigation throughout Antarctica.

The South African Government extends its best wishes to the Conference in the assurance that its deliberations will be conducted in a constructive spirit so that we may achieve the goal we have set ourselves.

Conf. doc. 6, October 15, 1959

Statement by Mr. McIntosh (*New Zealand*)

On behalf of the New Zealand delegation, I should like to express our appreciation of the welcome extended to us this morning by the Secretary of State.

9

If the arrangements and hospitality offered by the United States Government can be regarded as an augury, we can be assured of a successful conference.

In making this statement on behalf of my Prime Minister, Mr. Walter Nash, I have been asked to convey to other delegates his deep regret at not being able to be present for the opening of the Conference, and to state his views.

This regret is all the keener by reason of the fact that Mr. Nash has for many years taken, and continues to take, a day to day interest in proposals for joint international action in respect of Antarctica.

New Zealand has, in recent years, advocated international action to ensure the future use of Antarctica for the welfare of all nations.

As other delegates will no doubt be aware, Mr. Nash has made it clear that the New Zealand Government, for its part, would be prepared to consider the relinquishment of national rights and claims in Antarctica if such a step towards the establishment of a wider regime were generally agreed.

This does not mean that New Zealand is in any sense doubtful about the validity of its title to the Ross Dependency, or is unwilling to maintain its responsibilities for the administration of that area.

New Zealand's claim to the Ross Dependency is firmly grounded upon a substantial record of early British exploration in Antarctica, beginning with the great voyage of discovery of Captain Cook in the southern oceans. It was Cook who first used New Zealand's essential base and staging facilities; and for nearly two centuries since many other Antarctic explorers have met their staging needs in New Zealand. The area over which New Zealand claims jurisdiction was the scene of intensive exploratory work by Sir James Clark Ross between 1839 and 1843 and by the expeditions of Scott, Shackleton and other British parties at the beginning of the present century.

Since jurisdiction over the Dependency was formally transferred to New Zealand by the United Kingdom in 1923, legal title has been supported by administrative acts to regulate whaling and other activities in the territory, and in more recent years by further exploratory and scientific expeditions.

This is a brief record of the basis of the New Zealand claim, which we are confident will stand the closest scrutiny. In saying this I am of course aware that other countries with claims as well as those which have not made or recognized claims can advance substantial arguments about their national interests in Antarctica.

But, in this issue, it is not enough to adhere to past attitudes. This is why my Prime Minister has put forward the view that the establishment of a completely international regime for Antarctica would require countries to forego their national claims.

In Mr. Nash's view, it is only on this basis that a fully effective administration of the whole of Antarctica could be achieved—an administration which could coordinate all activities and ensure the permanent neutralization of the area. Such an international regime could prepare for the eventual use of the resources of Antarctica in a regulated and orderly manner.

New Zealand would, as Mr. Nash has also publicly stated, envisage the establishment of an organic relationship between such an Antarctic regime and the United Nations, in the belief that joint international action in Antarctica could provide a practical demonstration of the principles for which the United Nations stands.

The New Zealand Government recognizes, however, that at the present time it may not be possible to secure general agreement to an Antarctic settlement of this scope and nature.

Accordingly, while this broader concept remains the basis of the New Zealand approach to Antarctic problems, the New Zealand Government is prepared to join in more limited discussions, directed towards specific objectives on which a general measure of agreement is possible.

The convening of the present Conference suggests that there is in fact a widespread—and most welcome—willingness to discuss specific problems affecting international cooperation in Antarctica.

Although the whole world will benefit in due course from the comprehensive and fascinating exploration of our environment known as the International Geophysical Year, the twelve countries represented at this Conference have particular reason to acknowledge the value of the I.G.Y.

That experiment in global scientific cooperation has had, in respect of Antarctica, a two-fold result. It has provided a precedent for similar cooperation on an intergovernmental level. At the same time it has shown the need for such cooperation.

The New Zealand delegation at this Conference would wish to see a Treaty concluded which would meet four main objectives:

(1) It should provide a basis for avoiding rivalries and quarrels over territorial claims and conflicting national interests in Antarctica.

(2) It should ensure that Antarctica remains permanently "sealed off" from the tensions of the Cold War and free from war or the threat of war.

11

(3) It should assist continuing cooperation in scientific activities in Antarctica, and affirm the principle of the widest freedom of access to Antarctica for peaceful purposes.

(4) It should be associated with the United Nations in an appropriate manner.

As I have already mentioned, the New Zealand Government believes that the only final solution to territorial disputes and rivalries may eventually prove to be an agreement to relinquish national rights and claims in respect of Antarctica.

Since this is clearly not possible at the present time, the New Zealand delegation would for its part accept a simple arrangement to "freeze" the existing legal status quo as a way of ensuring that peaceful cooperation can continue unhampered by such disputes and rivalries.

There will surely also be general agreement on the need to keep Antarctica free from any form of militarization or warlike preparations.

It is accordingly our confident hope that this principle will be stated in treaty form, with provision also for methods of ensuring that the principle is scrupulously observed.

In particular, the New Zealand Government would wish to make quite clear its opposition to any nuclear testing or other testing of weapons in the Antarctic area.

We trust that it will also prove possible to agree on political arrangements to safeguard the excellent cooperative relationships already established in the scientific field.

New Zealand believes that such cooperation should be extended on the widest possible basis, with the sole qualification of an insistence that only activities directed towards peaceful purposes should be permitted.

In this manner, the New Zealand delegation considers that the nations at this Conference can demonstrate that there is nothing exclusive or restrictive about our motives in considering the future of Antarctica.

Treaty provisions of the kind I have suggested would be fully in accordance with the principles and purposes of the United Nations, to which all the states participating in the Conference have subscribed.

The New Zealand Government considers that in any treaty which is drawn up there should be specific recognition of the relationship which it would wish to see established with the United Nations. My delegation will have some detailed suggestions to offer to the Conference on this question.

We believe that these are objectives which all governments throughout the world would support; but the twelve countries participating in this Conference have a special role to play in achieving them.

They include all those states which have existing rights or claims in Antarctica, and all those other states at present active there.

This Conference should accordingly be able to give a lead to the world by agreeing to remove from Antarctica the conditions in which rivalries flourish and tensions develop. We must, moreover, keep in mind the responsibilities we owe to the rest of the world.

There will no doubt be differences of view. There will naturally be difficulties in reaching agreement on a Treaty which all can regard as satisfactory.

In seeking solutions of the problems confronting this Conference, we cannot do better than remind ourselves of the manner in which the tremendous physical hardships and difficulties of the Antarctic Continent have over the years been met and conquered by the great explorers of many nations.

Antarctica gives us a unique opportunity to take an initiative which could offer a hopeful prospect for similar cooperative relationships in other and more troubled areas of the world.

This vast and icy waste of 6,000,000 square miles, lying more in darkness than in light, has no permanent inhabitants. It can be explored and developed only with the resources of our advanced civilization. Its animosities, generated from outside, are potential rather than historic. It is only now being threatened by the tensions and rivalries that disturb the peace of the world elsewhere. As we see it the immediate task is to prevent such difficulties from developing and to let Antarctica remain in that peaceful state which, ironically, is the characteristic of areas unknown to man.

The leaders of the Great Powers have in recent weeks given encouraging indications of their desire for peace, and have declared their willingness to seek a general improvement in international relations.

It is my Prime Minister's earnest hope and that of the New Zealand Government and people that this Conference on Antarctica will provide a demonstration of what can be done—despite considerable difficulties and natural hesitations—when there is the need and the will to cooperate.

Statement by Mr. Asakai (*Japan*)

First of all I want to offer my congratulations to our Chairman, Mr. Phleger, on his election to that post. I hope to see smooth sailing for this conference and a safe arrival in port with him as our pilot.

I would like to express my gratitude to the Honorable Secretary of State of the United States for the opening speech in which he welcomed us so warmly. Mr. Herter inspires us with a hopeful confidence in the noble and significant cause of this conference.

The need for international cooperation in Antarctica is of great significance. The Government of the United States has acted most happily for all countries concerned by inviting our attention to this need. I'm sure I speak for all of us when I say we are grateful to the United States Government for convening this conference here in Washington at this time.

I would also like to pay high tribute to the members of the preliminary conference. Thanks to their painstaking spadework our task is made smoother; the promise of ultimate success is brighter.

Now, Mr. Chairman, I would like to speak a few words about the policies and the fundamental thinking of my Government on the subject of this conference.

You all know, of course, how Japan secluded herself from the world for a long time. You know also that it was only in the middle of the last century that Japan opened her doors to foreign friendship and commerce. Only fifty years after this, the Japanese people began to show their interest in Antarctica.

From 1910 through 1912 a Japanese expedition under Captain Shirase explored the Ross Sea and areas adjacent to it as far south as the 80 degrees of latitude. Since 1934 our fleets have been actively engaged in whaling operations there, except for their suspension during the war years. More recently we have dispatched scientific expeditions to Antarctica every year since 1956 under the International Geophysical Year program.

I wish to point out here that, despite all this activity in the area, never in her history has Japan made territorial claim to any part of Antarctica. Logically Japan might have taken advantage of the achievements of the Shirase expedition to institute political claims, but it has never been our intention to do so, even without the provisions of Article 2 of the San Francisco Peace Treaty.[1]

---

[1] For the text of the Treaty of Peace with Japan, signed on Sept. 8, 1951, see *Treaties and Other International Acts Series* 2490 (3 UST, pt. 3, p. 3169) ; also printed in *American Foreign Policy, 1950–1955: Basic Documents* (Department of State publication 6446), vol. I, pp. 425–440.

Nevertheless, the Japanese people have consistently entertained a deep attachment to and a keen interest in Antarctica and they still do. The Showa Base on the coast of Prince Harald could not have been established successfully without the united and powerful support of the entire nation of Japan.

Our experience leads the people and the Government of Japan earnestly to hope that Antarctica will be used for peaceful purposes only without being subject to the conflicts and disturbances of world politics. The invitation to the conference to conclude a treaty on Antarctica, issued by the United States Government in May of last year,[1] was in complete harmony with the aspirations of the people and the Government of Japan. For this reason my Government accepted that invitation whole-heartedly, along with the other ten countries.

As the invitation of the American Government says, our twelve countries have pursued useful international cooperation for scientific purposes in Antarctica under the International Geophysical Year project. The treaty we have in mind has as its main purpose to provide a legal basis for the existing structure of international cooperation and to ensure for the future that Antarctica will always and only be used for peaceful and scientific purposes and that it will be kept open for those purposes.

International cooperation such as we have effected under the International Geophysical Year program has no parallel in any other region of the world or in any other field of activity. We should be proud of this. At this moment, Mr. Chairman, I can think of no other example of such a wholehearted international cooperation, anywhere else in this strife-torn world. It is like a beacon on the road to world peace. We, here, must do our best to raise that beacon so it may throw its peaceful light on more and more of the world's peoples.

With this in mind, I submit that the freedom to use Antarctica for peaceful purposes and scientific research, which it is the chief purpose of our Treaty to ensure, should not be monopolized by these twelve countries. To achieve our principal purpose most effectively it is essential that we keep the Treaty open for accession by all countries which have a bona fide interest in Antarctica and which are willing to subscribe to the conditions of our Treaty.

Another factor that calls for our attention is this: the drafting of our Treaty on Antarctica involves a number of entirely novel elements in the realm of the existing principles of international law. The freezing of territorial claims on Antarctica, the complex composition of Antarctica, the nonmilitarization of Antarctica and observation and inspection for that purpose, criminal and civil jurisdiction in Antarc-

---

[1] See *ante*, pp. 2–4.

tica—these are among the questions difficult of regulation on the basis of the concepts of international law we now know.

Take for example the question of the zone of application of our Treaty. Research under the International Geophysical Year program shows that the Antarctic continent is composed of small areas of exposed land, large expanses permanently covered with ice, and some areas seasonally frozen. Not only the limits of these several areas, but even the border lines of the whole Antarctic region cannot presently be established scientifically. Neither do we know if the soil bed under the permanent ice lies above sea level or below. How do we apply to these complex actualities our established ideas of international law relating to territorial waters, inland waters, the high seas?

Also, to establish Antarctica as a completely nonmilitary area under proper observation and inspection poses a real challenge. It will be the first time in history such an attempt has been made on so large a scale and in an area so sparsely populated. Should we succeed here, we provide a hopeful precedent for the solution of one of the most important problems now facing the whole world.

With these points in mind, I submit that we have to make a totally flexible approach in grappling with the task of drafting our Treaty on Antarctica, and I want to assure you, Mr. Chairman, that the Japanese delegation participates in the deliberations throughout this conference with a very flexible and open-minded attitude.

The Government and the people of Japan earnestly and confidently hope that this conference will exhibit fully the spirit of peaceful cooperation already attained by our twelve countries relative to Antarctica. We hope this conference will conclude such a treaty as will in future be a model of international cooperation in other fields of activity.

Conf. doc. 8 (Rev. 1) (Corrected), October 17, 1959

Statement by Mr. Mora (*Chile*)

I should like first of all on behalf of the Chilean Delegation, to congratulate the distinguished Ambassador, Mr. Herman Phleger, on his appointment as Chairman of this Conference. For our part, we rejoice that the proposal we made in favor of Ambassador Phleger was unanimously accepted, for we are certain that, with his experience and wisdom as a jurist and diplomat, he will be able to lead our discussions skillfully and surely along the pathway of success.

It is with the deepest interest that Chile joins in the important work of this Conference, and therefore my country offers its fullest

16

cooperation in attaining the lofty objectives that inspired President Eisenhower to convoke it.

This interest in the Antarctic Continent on the part of Chile is certainly not something of today or yesterday. It goes back to the days, now far remote, when shortly after the Republic was established the country was able, to the extent of its capabilities, to broaden and strengthen its activities of all kinds in those regions.

This Conference has before it, therefore, a task that is undoubtedly of transcendental importance—that of clarifying as far as possible what has been termed the Antarctic problem, a complex problem, since it involves at the same time scientific, economic, strategic, and political aspects.

From a geographic standpoint I wish to emphasize a well-known fact: my country is the closest one to the Antarctic Continent, for between the Antarctic Continent and its southernmost insular possessions in the Americas the distance is hardly more than 428 nautical miles, clear proof that the southern extreme of the American hemisphere and the Antarctic Continent of today were joined together in another age.

The government of Chile considers that the Chilean Antarctic sector, the limits of which were fixed by Supreme Decree No. 1747 of November 6, 1940, which I had the honor to sign during the Aguirre Cerda administration [1] in my capacity as Minister of Foreign Relations at the time, forms an integral part of the territory of the nation and constitutes a natural extension thereof toward the South Pole.

From a political standpoint, my government fully shares the view of the host government that the Antarctic problem must not be linked with other problems of today, but rather must be faced with realism and with respect for territorial sovereignties, because I take the liberty of saying that our Antarctic regions formed a part of the Chilean domain a long time before our country won its independence in 1810.

In this connection, the reply which my government had the honor to give to the invitation to attend this Conference stated that the case of Chile presents distinctive characteristics because the Chilean Antarctic territory does not have the character of a colonial possession but is part of its metropolitan territory and forms part of its southernmost province. It was added on the above-mentioned occasion that Chile saw two distinct basic objectives in the invitation: one, of a scientific type, and the other, of a political nature. With respect to the first [second?], it was stated in advance that Chile could not ac-

---

[1] Pedro Aguirre Cerda was President of the Republic of Chile, December 1938–November 1941.

cept any formula that might imply the internationalization of its Antarctic territory because that would be contrary to the normal exercise of its sovereignty and would contravene clearly stated provisions of its Constitution.

Our Foreign Office also stated that it viewed with satisfaction the aim to continue the scientific cooperation set up on the occasion of the International Geophysical Year, but that it should be continued in conformity with the principles and procedures agreed upon at that time.

With regard to the second objective, Chile is not opposed to the possibility of studying an international commitment aimed at guaranteeing the peaceful use of the Antarctic Continent but rather much to the contrary, in accordance with its traditional peaceful policy, will gladly cooperate to that end. But it fears that an agreement of this nature may weaken the provisions of the Inter-American Treaty of Reciprocal Assistance signed at Rio de Janeiro in 1947 [4] if the necessary precautions are not taken. As we know, part of the American Antarctic is included within the "Continental Security Zone" created by the said Treaty for which reason Chile considers that it would be advisable to state in the pertinent part that the provisions of the Antarctic Treaty in no way affect the principles contained in the aforementioned international instrument.

Lastly, my government suggested in its reply that it would be useful to supplement those objectives with an agreement on the conservation of the Antarctic maritime resources.

The government of Chile also thinks that the diplomatic instrument or instruments resulting from this meeting should, in their final wording, be as specific as possible and consider complications that might arise with respect to other international agreements into which we have entered. For example, it is well to reflect carefully on whether such an Antarctic agreement will enter the sphere of the so-called "Regional Agreements" referred to in Chapter VIII of the United Nations Charter, or whether it will better fall within another type of international pact. The question is important in our opinion, and it is therefore our obligation not to avoid giving a specific pronouncement in this connection.

We could make other observations regarding certain ideas that were exchanged in the preliminary stage of this meeting; we also could dwell more extensively, as some other Delegates have done, on detailed considerations concerning the bases of various kinds that lend special

---

[4] For text, see *Treaties and Other International Acts Series* 1838 (62 Stat., pt. 2, p. 1681) ; also printed in *Department of State Bulletin*, Sept. 21, 1947, pp. 565–567.

strength to our claims and rights concerning the portion of the Antarctic Territory that belongs to us; but my Delegation prefers to avail itself of the opportunity to express those observations and arguments in the course of the discussions to come, as a constructive contribution to the greater success of this Conference, which is starting today under such favorable auspices.

I do not wish to conclude without expressing our sincere gratitude for the cordial hospitality given our Delegation by the government of the United States, and our conviction that our deliberations and decisions must be inspired by the concept which the countries of our hemisphere expressed in one of their most significant periodical meetings: "Peace is the fulfillment of Justice sustained by the moral order and having the guarantee of Law."

Conf. doc. 9, October 15, 1959

Statement by Mr. Koht (*Norway*)

First of all I want to thank the Secretary of State for his kind words of welcome.

Norway has during the years been actively engaged in the polar regions, both for reasons of exploration and pure science, and not least have those parts of the world afforded us considerable economic support. It is sufficient to draw the attention to the Norwegian whaling fleet, which, since the beginning of this century, has been active in the waters of Antarctica and which was the main reason for Norwegian presence in the area.

There should be no need to remind anyone of the achievements of the distinguished explorer Roald Amundsen, who, together with four other Norwegians, was the first to set foot on the geographic South Pole on December 14th, 1911, planting the Norwegian flag there and naming the area Haakon the Seventh's plateau. Numerous other expeditions from Norway visited that area of Antarctica which was later to be named Queen Maud Land, during the thirties. The most prominent of these expeditions were under the sponsorship of Lars Christensen, one of the pioneers of international whaling.

These accomplishments, as well as those of expeditions from other nations, are the more remarkable when we consider the tremendous difficulties the pioneers of Antarctic exploration had to overcome. Some lost their lives in this world of ice and snow. I wish to pay tribute to those men of different nationalities who were the predecessors of today's scientists and explorers in these same regions.

Things have changed. The advanced technical civilization of the present day has made it possible to launch large-scale scientific operations in Antarctica, which little by little is yielding its secrets. Thus, time has clearly come for a new era to break in this vast continent, an era of international cooperation and mutual understanding in order to solve those problems which will naturally and inevitably arise where nations with different backgrounds and experiences are actively engaged in the same field. In Antarctica this aim should be the easier to reach as we all would have one common interest: that of securing the peaceful development of the continent.

I want to extend my Government's thanks and appreciation for the initiative taken by the President of the United States in inviting the nations which have a principal interest in the area to participate in a conference with a view to establish an international arrangement for Antarctica. In the invitation three main principles for the future arrangement are outlined, viz:

1) International cooperation and coordination of scientific research,

2) Antarctica is to be used for purely peaceful purposes only, and

3) the legal status quo in Antarctica should be frozen for the duration of the arrangement reached, as far as rights and claims to territorial sovereignty are concerned. The Government of Norway in its reply to the United States' invitation expressed its willingness to participate in a conference as proposed and also its adherence to the basic principles which the United States had outlined.

I am happy to be able to say that Norway already has had the opportunity to practice international cooperation in the field of Antarctic scientific research. Starting in 1949 and terminating in 1952 a scientific team consisting of several nationalities [1] under Norwegian leadership built and manned "Maudheim", the name given to their headquarters in Queen Maud Land. The scientific knowledge gathered by their activities was considerable.

Norway Station, which is our IGY-station, and which is also situated in Queen Maud Land, is to be discontinued from the beginning of next year. Some time ago the Norwegian Government offered to lend this station to the Union of South Africa, and negotiations are taking place in this connection. It is hoped that it will prove possible to have the station manned by scientists from the Union of South Africa when our expedition is withdrawn. I can assure our South-African friends that Norway takes great pleasure in being able to assist the cause of science in this way.

To end let me express the hope that the conference which we now are about to begin will be successful and that we shall be able to reach

---

[1] Norwegian-British-Swedish Antarctic expedition, 1949–52.

those aims we have set in order to further a peaceful and orderly development in the future of Antarctica.

As far as Norway is concerned, we promise to do our utmost to succeed in what we all are now about to undertake.

AFTERNOON MEETING (3:00–4:30 p.m.)

Mr. Phleger, Presiding

Conf. doc. 10, October 16, 1959

Statement by Mr. Kuznetsov (*Soviet Union*)

Allow me, on behalf of the Soviet delegation, to express our greetings to the representatives of the countries assembled here at the Conference on Antarctica.

The present Conference has been convened to discuss important questions concerning Antarctica and to work out an international treaty which would contribute to the further development of fruitful cooperation among states in this part of the globe.

It is known that Antarctica is a vast area in the center of our planet, a continent with a territory surpassing that of Europe in size.

At present when we stand on the threshold of man's penetration into outer space we still have considerable gaps in our knowledge about the nature of our planet. Of vast area, Antarctica has not yet revealed all its secrets. This makes more difficult the solution of major geophysical problems on a world scale. The solution of these problems, however, would permit even wider use of the forces of nature for the benefit of mankind.

The economic potential of the Antarctic continent has not yet been sufficiently studied, but there is reason to believe that in the future, in conjunction with a more detailed exploration of Antarctica and the development of means of communication, this continent will be of still greater importance. The Antarctic waters are abundant in organic sea life and intensive fishing is carried on there, accounting for about 9/10 of the total world catch of whales.

Having in mind the geographic, economic, historic and other conditions, the Soviet Government has always proceeded from the premise that it is expedient to settle the question of the régime for Antarctica on an international basis with a view to attaining an agreement that would respond to the legitimate interests of all states. It is known that the Soviet Government has moved to invite to the Conference on

Antarctica all the states which might wish to take part. The participation of the greatest possible number of states in the treaty under consideration would contribute to its effectiveness.

At this Conference those states are represented that are at present directly conducting scientific research in Antarctica. The convening of an International Conference on Antarctica is, undoubtedly, a positive factor, and it may play a substantial role in the further development of international cooperation in this area of the world.

The convening of this Conference indicates that its participants agree that a régime for Antarctica should be established on an international basis with due consideration to mutual interests and rights.

Our Conference is the first in history held on Antarctica, the exploration of which began many years ago. It should lay the foundation for an international régime of Antarctica.

In the view of the Soviet Government, the Conference in working out an international treaty must proceed on the basis of the main task now facing mankind. This task is to maintain and consolidate peace among all states, to develop and strengthen friendship among all nations.

Proceeding from the above, the Soviet Government considers that there should be established in Antarctica an international régime that would contribute to the strengthening of peace and would exclude the possibility of this area being turned into a source of frictions and tensions in the relations between states.

Therefore, it is important, first of all, to come to an agreement providing for the use of Antarctica for peaceful purposes only. This means that the carrying out in Antarctica of any measures of military nature, in particular the construction of military bases and installations, the conducting of military, naval and air exercises and the testing of any types of weapons, should be prohibited.

The conclusion of an international treaty will, undoubtedly, open up the prospects for a more effective exploration of that region.

Gentlemen, Russia has made a great contribution to the common cause of exploration of Antarctica. As is known, its navigators and scientists, Bellingshausen and Lazarev, were the first to discover the sixth continent at the beginning of the Nineteenth Century.[1]

The Soviet Union is taking an active part in the exploration of Antarctica by conducting extensive research there. The work that has been assigned to Soviet scientists concerns the exploration of those almost inaccessible areas of the Antarctic continent, namely, its hinterland, of which mankind knew nothing until recently.

---

[1] This refers to the voyage of Adm. Thaddeus von Bellingshausen, accompanied by Lt. Mikhail Petrovich Lazarev, in the *Mirny* and *Vostok*, 1819–21.

Soviet explorers penetrated into those regions of the Antarctic continent that lie furthest from the coast, they reached the South geomagnetic pole and the pole of relative inaccessibility and stayed in these regions during winter periods. They discovered the pole of cold of our planet where an air temperature of 87.6° below zero centigrade was registered.

The Soviet scientists were working under unusually difficult conditions, which were to a certain extent similar to those expected in outer space where much exploration has already been done by Soviet scientists as well as by scientists of other countries.

The selfless work of Soviet explorers in Antarctica gives valuable scientific data, which becomes available to the scientists of all countries.

The Soviet scientists, naturally, realize that the results of their research work constitute only a part of what has recently been done by all of the scientists working in Antarctica.

We are glad to note that in Antarctica—this coldest region of our planet—exceptionally warm relations have developed between scientists from different countries. A wide exchange of the results of research work and observations, close contacts between expeditions, unselfish aid and mutual assistance in surmounting difficulties—these are characteristic features of scientific cooperation in Antarctica. It may be said without exaggeration that, as a result of this international scientific cooperation, mankind has learned more about Antarctica in the last three or four years than in all the 130 years since the day of its discovery.

To ensure still closer and wider international cooperation it is necessary to consolidate the existing principle of freedom of scientific exploration in Antarctica. This principle, which has gained general recognition in the carrying out of the International Geophysical Year, means that governments, organizations and citizens of all countries may conduct scientific research in Antarctica on the basis of equality.

As to the question of the territorial claims in Antarctica, the position of the Soviet Union was laid down in the Soviet Government's note of June 2, 1958, which stated in particular:

> The Soviet Union reserves for itself all of the rights based on the discoveries and explorations of Russian seafarers and scientists, including the right to make appropriate territorial claims in Antarctica.

Realizing the complex and delicate character of the territorial problems in Antarctica, the Soviet Union supports the agreement on this question arrived at in the course of the preliminary negotiations which took place in connection with preparations for this Conference.

Fellow Delegates, at present favorable conditions are emerging in the world for more active cooperation of all states in the interests of consolidating universal peace and security. The historic visit of the Chairman of the Council of Ministers of the U.S.S.R., N. S. Khrushchev, to the United States of America[1] and his talks with the U.S. President, Dwight D. Eisenhower, was an important contribution to the improvement of the international situation.

Our Conference is meeting at a time when the trend towards warmer relations between states is discernible, and, figuratively speaking, this fair wind that has appeared in the international atmosphere is favorable for our Conference and must assist in the happy sailing of our ship.

Mr. Chairman, Gentlemen, as is known, since June of last year preliminary negotiations between representatives of the states participating in this Conference have been held in Washington, during which a considerable amount of work has been done.

We note with satisfaction that these negotiations were conducted in a spirit of business-like cooperation and mutual understanding. The Soviet delegation expresses its hope that this constructive cooperation will continue also at the Conference that opened today.

Availing myself of this opportunity, I would like to express our appreciation of the efforts of the Government of the United States in convening this Conference and to thank Secretary of State Christian Herter for his warm words of welcome spoken here.

The Soviet delegation hopes that this Conference will successfully solve the tasks facing it, will work out an international treaty on Antarctica, which will be in harmony with the aims and spirit of the U.N. Charter, and will promote to the maximum extent the peaceful cooperation of states in this area.

For its part, the Soviet Government will make every effort to contribute to the success of the Conference.

Conf. doc. 11, October 15, 1959

Statement by Mr. Casey (*Australia*)

I first wish to express my thanks to Mr. Herter for his kind words of welcome and to say that the Australian Government greatly appreciates the American Government's invitation to hold this Conference in Washington.

I fully agree that this Conference for the settlement of Antarctic problems is one of the most promising developments in recent history, and if it is brought to a successful conclusion it will constitute an important and indeed a unique step forward in international relations.

---

[1] Sept. 15–27, 1959.

I must confess that when informal negotiations were first begun over a year ago for an Antarctic Treaty, the Australian Government was not optimistic that a satisfactory basis of agreement could be found among all the countries with interests in the Antarctic. These countries are very diverse in their own national backgrounds and in the past have tended to follow different courses in the Antarctic. In fact, in some cases there have been direct conflicts of national interest. It seemed unlikely therefore that sufficient common ground could be found to provide the basis for an Antarctic Treaty. The Australian Government believed that unless such common ground could be found it would be unwise to call a Conference. This would have raised unfounded hopes and might well have sharpened rather than diminished existing conflicts of interest. From the outset of the informal negotiations we therefore urged strongly that all Governments should seek a basic measure of agreement before calling a formal conference.

The Australian Government has been glad to find that, contrary to its earlier expectations, an important and valuable area of common agreement has been established among the twelve governments represented at this Conference. Although the informal discussions which have preceded the Conference are not necessarily binding on Governments, they have nevertheless enabled our representatives to define and formulate substantial agreement in all the important fields. I would go so far as to say that if all the informal understandings arrived at in the Working Group are upheld by the delegations to this Conference, the successful conclusion of the Treaty is assured.

The Leaders of Delegations who have already spoken have presented in eloquent terms the broad principles on which it is hoped the Antarctic Treaty will be based. I need only say that the Australian Government is in full accord with these principles. We have for many years favoured the widest possible scientific cooperation in the area and the fullest exchange of scientific information. We have always made the information which we have acquired through our own activities in the Antarctic freely available to the rest of the world. We also emphatically endorse the principle that the whole of the Antarctic region should be reserved for peaceful uses only—and that no dispute of any kind shall be allowed to disturb the pax Antarctica. I might say that the more completely this principle is applied the happier the Australian Government will be. We are confident that all parties will pledge themselves to the principle that there should be no militarization of the Antarctic and I also am encouraged to believe that agreement will be reached on arrangements for observation and inspection which will ensure that this principle is carried out.

I believe that another important aspect of ensuring peace in the Antarctic is the elimination of potential causes of international rivalry and conflict. In the past the principal cause of such differences has been the question of territorial claims. It is therefore the Australian Government's profound conviction that everything possible should be done to eliminate this source of conflict. We realise that it would be optimistic to expect that the question of territorial claims could be settled at the present time. We have therefore come to the conclusion that the best solution is to include provisions in the Treaty which would preserve the status quo. This means that countries such as Australia who have made great efforts over many years in their own territories in the Antarctic will not be obliged to relinquish any of their rights and claims. At the same time we recognise that countries who have not made claims are entitled to maintain that their own position should not be worsened under the Treaty. I have been most gratified at the fact that in the informal discussions that have already taken place, general acceptance has been indicated of these concepts. I might in fact say that such acceptance has always been considered by the Australian Government as an essential prerequisite of a satisfactory treaty. It was only when it became clear that there was fairly general agreement on this point that we believed that the calling of a Conference was justified.

One of the primary objectives of the Treaty must be to eliminate suspicions in the Antarctic. I do not wish to imply that at the present time there are any such suspicions; in fact, in recent years co-operation in the area has been marked by the most complete international goodwill. We want to keep it that way. As realists we must recognise that as the importance of the area grows and as national activities continue to develop, the possibilities of disagreement are likely to increase. Only by signing a treaty on the lines at present contemplated can we keep the Antarctic from becoming a breeding ground for suspicion—which is the great corroder.

The Antarctic's geographical relationship with the Australian continent means that it is of special importance to us. Australia's southern coastline of 2000 miles runs parallel to the Antarctic coastline only 2000 or 3000 miles to the south. The weather of Australia is greatly affected by Antarctic meteorological conditions. As a country largely concerned with agricultural and pastoral production Australia has an important economic interest in a close knowledge of Antarctic weather conditions.

Australia has a long history of exploration and scientific activity in the Antarctic and the Australian territory makes up almost one-third of the continent. In the nineteenth century a number of Australians participated in exploration and whaling activity in the region. In 1909 two of the three members of Sir Ernest Shackleton's expedition who reached the South Magnetic Pole were Australians. These were Sir Douglas Mawson and Sir Edgeworth David whose names have since become famous in the annals of Antarctic exploration. Mawson led the Australasian Antarctic expedition of 1911/1914 which discovered and explored King George V and Queen Mary Lands, explored Adélie Land and sledged to the South Magnetic Pole area. He also led the British, Australian, New Zealand Antarctic Research Expedition of 1929/31. This expedition discovered MacRobertson Land and the BANZARE Coast, and visited Kemp and Enderby Lands.

Sir Hubert Wilkins, an Australian who spent many years of his life in the United States, went on expeditions to the Antarctic several times and explored Graham Land from the air in 1928–30. During 1934–37 another Australian, John Rymill, led the British Graham Land Expedition which discovered and surveyed much of the coast of Graham Land and its off-lying islands.

Australian post-war Antarctic activities began in the summer of 1947–48, when the Australian National Antarctic Research Expedition under the leadership of Stuart Campbell made a reconnaissance of the coast-line of King George V Land in the "Wyatt Earp". In December, 1947 a scientific research station was established on Heard Island, and another one on Macquarie Island in March 1948.

Since 1953 the Australian National Antarctic Research Expedition under the direction of Phillip Law, has carried out extensive exploration along the coast of the Australian Antarctic Territory. It is now true to say that practically the whole of the coastline of the Australian sector has been explored and photographed from the air.

In February 1954 our first permanent base on the Antarctic mainland, Mawson, was set up in MacRobertson Land. In January 1957, a second mainland base, Davis, was established in the Vestfold Hills area, and in January 1958, an automatic weather station was set up on Lewis Island, just to the west of the French territory of Adélie Land.

In February 1959 the Australians took over operation of the Wilkes Station which had been established by the United States on the Budd Coast.

Australia is most conscious of the importance of scientific research in the Antarctic. I have already mentioned the effect of Antarctic meteorology on Australia but we are also deeply interested in many other fields of scientific endeavour. I would like to mention, I hope with all proper modesty, that Australia may be regarded as one of the six or eight most advanced scientific nations in the world. We have made important contributions to scientific development in a number of fields and are already equipped to develop our research in several important directions. Research in the Antarctic will be an important complement to these efforts. This is particularly true in such fields as geophysics, geomagnetism, cosmic rays and the ionosphere. I would emphasize that scientific data of great importance to research workers studying the upper atmosphere can be gained from observations in the Antarctic. Such work has recently been greatly stimulated by the remarkable discoveries of Van Allen [1] and others of zones of intense radiation which exist in doughnut form near the earth. The holes in these doughnuts are above the geomagnetic polar regions—which may be of significance as scientific effort develops.

Another aspect of Antarctic research which may be of great ultimate importance to the rest of the world is the study of the nutritive wealth of the Antarctic seas. In view of the astronomical increase in the world demand for food that is likely to occur within the next fifty years it is quite conceivable that mankind will have to turn to the Antarctic zones as a source of protein food for both animals and human beings.

Work in a number of scientific disciplines is carried out at our four main bases—at Macquarie Island, Mawson, Davis and Wilkes, and in the field. The Australian base at Heard Island was closed down in March 1955, when our scientific research work there was completed. In addition, our automatic weather station on Lewis Island is of considerable interest and scientific usefulness.

Australia has of course participated fully in the work of the Special Committee on Antarctic Research (SCAR) [2] and considerable scientific work on the Antarctic is carried out in Australia under the auspices of this organization. The permanent Secretary of the Working Group on Cartography is an Australian and the function of this group is to co-ordinate information about mapping of the Antarctic to prevent unnecessary duplication of effort. At the invitation of SCAR Australia has also set up the International Antarctic Weather Analysis Centre in Melbourne.

In view of our efforts in the Antarctic over several decades, I feel that I am justified in claiming that Australia has made an important contribution to the opening up of this difficult and inhospitable con-

---

[1] Dr. James Alfred Van Allen, professor and head of Physics Department, State University of Iowa.

[2] Special Committee on Antarctic Research, established by the International Council of Scientific Unions to meet the need for further international organization of scientific activity in Antarctica beyond the IGY.

tinent. We have not however engaged in these activities solely in our national interest. We have always sought to share with others the results of our efforts. We co-operated wholeheartedly in the International Geophysical Year and we fully support one of the main objectives of the proposed Antarctic Treaty, which is to facilitate the continuation and expansion of international scientific co-operation in the area. There is nothing exclusive about the proposed Treaty. The twelve countries gathered at this conference are the ones with direct interests and responsibilities in the area and it is right and proper that they should have the task of drawing up a treaty for the area. As far as Australia is concerned however we do not believe that membership of such a treaty need necessarily be limited to the present twelve. For example, any member of the United Nations who is prepared to undertake the considerable effort of maintaining operations in the Antarctic area should perhaps be able to join the Treaty. But even those countries who do not join it will stand to benefit greatly from it. Apart from the world-wide importance of the establishment of an area of permanent peace in the Antarctic, the whole world will benefit from the scientific co-operation among the signatories to the Treaty.

I would therefore like to say in conclusion, Mr. Chairman, that if this conference succeeds in drawing up a treaty for the Antarctic it will be of very great benefit not only to the signatories but to the whole of mankind.

Conf. doc. 12, October 15, 1959;
Corr. 1, October 21, 1959

Statement by Mr. Charpentier (*France*)

Mr. Chairman, it is a joy for me to be able to express publicly the cordial thanks of my Government for the reception accorded us in Washington and for the words of welcome you have addressed to us.

The step taken by the Government of the United States—and I should like to stress it at this time—appears to us extremely felicitous.

The Antarctic portion of the work of the International Geophysical Year was carried out in an atmosphere of understanding and harmony, untroubled by any rivalry. The pathway of scientific cooperation among nations on which this experience has started us is full of promise. It would have been most regrettable if such an effort had not been followed up, and we congratulate ourselves on the agreement reached by the interested governments to strengthen the results obtained and to extend into the future an activity as fruitful as this has been.

The French Government, which has already furnished proof of its intentions in that regard, is ready to give its full assistance to the development of scientific cooperation among nations with respect to the Antarctic Continent. It sees in the emulation of the courageous explorers who, despite the harshness of the climate, are working together to increase the sum total of human knowledge, a shining example of what can be accomplished by good understanding among nations.

France has been in the forefront of the countries that are engaged in scientific cooperation in the Antarctic. It takes pride in this and intends to continue its work. It actively participated in the work of the Scientific Committee on Antarctic Research since that body was established and its scientists are keeping in close touch with the foreign scientific missions that have undertaken the study of the southern continent. It is willing to increase its efforts in that field.

Military neutralization of the Antarctic regions, which the Conference proposes to bring about, also meets with the full approval of my country. The French expeditions in the Antarctic have never served to support any activity of a military nature, and the programs drawn up for the next few years in that region of the world are concerned only with the development of scientific research. We agree that controlled military neutralization of the Antarctic should be instituted in the form of a convention and should be the subject of solemn commitments on the part of all interested governments.

France attaches all the more importance to the work of the Conference, since for many years it has been represented on the southern seas and in the Antarctic. Its sovereignty over Adélie Land, discovered in 1840 by Dumont d'Urville who flew the tricolor there for the first time, explored by Charcot [1] at the beginning of this century, and crossed in recent years by the French polar expeditions, rests on solid foundations. The French Government is proud, in addition to having undisputable historical claims, to be able to rely on a permanent occupation which, if it affirms our rights, serves at the same time the higher interests of science.

Such are the reasons for which my country is anxious to express its satisfaction at taking part in the work which we are undertaking today; such are the reasons for which it expresses the hope of seeing this work succeed in the interest of cooperation among nations, and in the interest of science and of peace.

---

[1] Dr. Jean B. Charcot led French Antarctic expeditions in 1903–05 and in 1908–10.

Conf. doc. 13 (Rev. 1), November 5, 1959

Statement by Mr. Scilingo (*Argentina*)

The Conference that is opening today upon the invitation of the Government of the United States of America and at which the countries that participated in the activities of the International Geophysical Year are represented, has been convened to deal with the question of the exclusively peaceful use of and scientific cooperation in Antarctica.

The area that the discussions will cover includes a sector forming the subject of an Argentine-Chilean declaration of recognition of mutual rights, which, as a natural extension of the Argentine Republic, has, for many decades, formed an integral part of its territory. Argentina installed in Antarctica the first permanent observatory in 1904.[1] Since then, not to mention activities prior to that year, it has been establishing bases, stations, refuges, lighthouses, buoys, post offices, and radio-telegraph stations. Argentine military men and Argentine men of science have performed many deeds of heroism in the Antarctic wilderness and some have given their lives in the unceasing process of their outstanding technical and scientific work. Under those circumstances, Mr. Chairman, it can be a surprise to no one that Antarctica has taken root and established an awareness in the soul of the Argentine nation.

The Argentine Republic, the first actual and continuous occupant of the area, which has been incorporated administratively for some time into the Tierra del Fuego Government District, which is only a few hundred nautical miles from the Antarctic, is attending this Conference with all these rights. They indicate the measure of its interest in the discussions that are beginning and of the importance that it attaches to this Conference. They also determine its line of action and its responsibility.

This Conference—and it is fitting that we set forth these ideas clearly—has not been convened to institute régimes or to create structures. It is not its mission to change or alter anything. Nothing that is done here or is the consequence of what is agreed upon here will give rise, affect, or will disregard rights. The objective of this Conference is to reach an agreement, with the express concurrence of all the parties, upon the peaceful use of and scientific cooperation in the Antarctic area within the geographic boundary that may be agreed upon. With that clear understanding, Argentina will take part in the work with a sincere desire to cooperate.

---

[1] On Laurie Island in the South Orkney group.

The nuclear world in which we live, in which science, ever working wonders, is constantly producing new forms and instruments of massive destruction, would make the consequences of an armed conflict far worse than the human mind could conceive. War, and the danger or threat of war, have been casting their dark shadows over a humanity that is far from desiring its own holocaust; a humanity that knows that those same media that are conspiring against its existence, if used for peaceful purposes, would create possibilities for development that could radically transform its living conditions.

Recent events and the mutual public recognition by two statesmen of their sincere reciprocal desire for peace are tending to create a new atmosphere in which a new spirit could take root. In this situation, if this Conference solemnly agrees on the exclusively peaceful use of the geographic area coming within its jurisdiction, it will have accomplished, by that fact alone, a historic task. This would be the first great step toward the realization of the hopes of the world.

If, at the same time, it establishes scientific cooperation as an end in itself, applicable to the area where it was begun and carried out under conditions that made it perfectly possible during the International Geophysical Year, which was mentioned in calling the Conference, it will, in the opinion of the Argentine Delegation, have fully accomplished its objectives.

Argentina will support those principles, whether they take the form of a declaration or treaty. Both principles flow from its tradition and its history. To mention but one or two precedents, I should like to recall that several years ago Argentina pledged itself, along with two other countries taking part in the Conference, not to send warships south of parallel 60 and that it has scrupulously kept that commitment and is still doing so. In its broad exploratory work in the Antarctic region it has always practiced both general and scientific cooperation. For over fifty years it has often had the privilege of giving its support to technical expeditions in difficult situations and has felt itself more than repaid by the expressions of public gratitude.

The Argentine Delegation will make its points of view known in the Committees. There it will express its concurrence or disagreement with such proposals as may be submitted and it will present some of its own.

Mr. Chairman, if we should work wisely in a spirit of mutual understanding, we could, provided we rise above dissimilar interests and situations, reach a satisfactory agreement.

I sincerely hope that this will be accomplished and I pledge the loyal cooperation of the Delegation of which I have the honor to be Chairman.

Statement by Viscount Obert de Thieusies (*Belgium*)

The Belgian delegation is very happy to pay tribute to President Eisenhower's initiative in calling a conference of the interested powers with a view to preparing a provisional statute for the Antarctic. It considers this step a very concrete effort toward promoting international understanding and cooperation wherever possible.

The Antarctic has shown, in a field that is of course geographically limited but nevertheless vast, just how possible it is to cooperate in a very friendly spirit.

Belgium, whose Antarctic expedition of 1958 owes much to the spontaneous and generous aid of the Russians and Americans, is particularly aware of that fact.

Hence, it is a really enticing prospect—that of bringing together the powers that have knowledge of the Antarctic, the problems that arise there, and the difficulties that must be overcome there in order to establish and perpetuate, by a deliberative agreement, the spirit of understanding that has continually manifested itself with respect to the Antarctic. Those who have had to surmount the same obstacles are always ready to understand one another.

Belgium expresses the wish that the present negotiations will end in unanimous agreement, which would thus set an example that might be followed in other fields.

Belgium has the right to be invited to these sessions. It is proud of this. Its contribution to the scientific exploration of the Antarctic is not, as a matter of fact, entirely recent. The Adrien de Gerlache expedition of 1898 was the first to spend the winter within the polar circle; next month the fourth Belgian expedition will set out for this still mysterious continent. This expresses all the interest it has shown and will continue to show in the Antarctic. The Belgian delegation, therefore, wishes to emphasize that it is specifically in the name of that interest that it hopes the planned agreement will be successfully concluded.

Statement by Sir Esler Dening (*United Kingdom*)

Mr. Chairman, on behalf of the United Kingdom Delegation, I should like to express our warm thanks to Mr. Herter, Secretary of State of the United States, for presiding over the preliminary proceedings of this Conference and for his kind words of welcome to the Delegates. I should also like to congratulate you, Sir, on your election to your responsible office, just as we congratulate ourselves on having made available to us the benefits of your wisdom and your experience. We are grateful too to the U.S. Government for the facilities and organisation they have so kindly placed at our disposal for the smooth and speedy transaction of the business which lies before us. As to the nature of that business other distinguished Delegates have already made reference to the spirit of cooperation and the considerable measure of agreement achieved by the Working Group, and I should like to pay tribute to the extent of their accomplishment.

The U.K. Delegation approaches the present Conference in no rigid or inflexible spirit. Her Majesty's Government in the United Kingdom have for many years been in favour of the conclusion of an agreement between countries actively interested in the Antarctic, if only because of the peculiar and indeed unique conditions which prevail there, and because of the special nature of the benefits which mankind may expect to derive from the area. For these reasons, as long ago as 1948, they indicated their readiness to accept proposals put forward by the United States Government for an international regime in the Antarctic.[1] Ten years later, they welcomed equally the invitation of President Eisenhower, extended in May, 1958, to participate in this present Conference.

We are wholly in agreement with the United States as to the high value to be attached to the close international cooperation achieved during the International Geophysical Year in the Antarctic, and we warmly welcome the prospect of ensuring the continuance of the scientific cooperation which has already added measurably to our knowledge of this remote area of the earth's surface.

The object of the Conference which meets here today for the first time is, as we see it, to consider and agree upon the terms of a Treaty, which will not only promote continuing international cooperation in the field of scientific research in the Antarctic, but will facilitate such cooperation by eliminating, as far as lies in the power of the countries represented here, the possibility of political dispute, or military menace, which might otherwise impede or retard international progress in the search for knowledge.

Of the 12 countries who have a special interest in the conclusion of a Treaty for the purposes indicated, the United Kingdom has a long record of Antarctic exploration. We were amongst the first in this field, and also amongst the first to establish permanent settlements for scientific investigation and the regulation of whaling activities. The Antarctic Circle was first crossed by Captain Cook in 1773. From 1900 onwards many points in the Antarctic were occupied at various

---

[1] See *Department of State Bulletin*, Sept. 5, 1948, p. 301.

34

times by British wintering parties. Continuous occupation of a number of research stations started in 1944. Our first formal territorial claims to parts of the continent were made as long ago as 1841. Throughout the period a large number of major expeditions of discovery and research have set out from the United Kingdom and a vast corpus of knowledge relating to certain parts of Antarctica has been amassed and made public; all these records are freely available at the Scott Polar Research Institute in England. Our surveys have been made by pioneer efforts over land and on the ice as well as from the air, often in circumstances of great difficulty and danger.

In keeping with the continuity of our interest, United Kingdom sovereignty over the area in which our activities had been, and were to be displayed, was consolidated in 1908 and 1917. The fact that this sovereignty has since been contested by rival claims gives substance to one of the matters which this Conference expects to discuss.

While we fully maintain the indisputable rights to sovereignty to which the U.K. is entitled we recognise the need to ensure that knowledge of the Antarctic and freedom of access to it should not be limited by political considerations. We are accordingly prepared to subscribe to a clause in the Treaty which will maintain the legal *status quo* throughout the area of the Antarctic. Indeed we consider such a clause to be an essential part of the Treaty if its main aims are to be secured.

There are other Powers represented at this Conference who have rights and claims in other areas of the Antarctic. The suggestion is that the Treaty should provide full protection for the present juridical position of all the Powers concerned, while they, for their part, will accept the obligations involved by adherence to the Treaty as a whole. In this way it is hoped to ensure that, for the duration of the Treaty, political disputes arising from territorial claims can be avoided.

We come next to the important principle that the Antarctic should be used for peaceful purposes only. In our view the Treaty must contain provisions for ensuring that this principle is observed in practice, for while we have, of course, no reason to doubt the good faith of the parties signatory to it, the principle of non-militarisation is still so new in international practice, that it would surely be wise to eliminate from the outset, the possibility that the actions of one or other of the parties, including the United Kingdom, can give rise to doubt or suspicion amongst other Powers as to whether the principle is being observed. We hope, therefore, that approval will be given to proposals for a system of observation and inspection sufficient, in the special conditions prevailing in the Antarctic, to ensure that the basic purpose of preserving the area from military activities is achieved. At the same time it seems important to bear in mind the relevance of certain practical considerations. Antarctic expeditions already work under very difficult conditions, and we must not add to the burdens of climate and geography, by imposing unacceptable conditions in the Treaty. We have particularly in mind the need to limit requirements as regards the attachment of observers to expeditions and bases, as well as the possible need of certain countries to provide logistic support for their scientific expeditions from military sources. It would be difficult to ban such support, though it must be made clear that military personnel and equipment can only be employed for peaceful purposes.

There are two further matters which are not only of close concern to this Conference, but which may well require clarification for the benefit of other countries who are not parties to our present deliberations. The first concerns any organisation which may be set up under the 12-Power Treaty which we are now about to negotiate, and the second, which is interlinked with it, relates to participation by other Powers and access to the Antarctic by other nations of the world.

As to the first, the participants in this Conference other than the United States are those who accepted the invitation of the United States Government, and they include on the one hand the group of Powers having territorial rights or claims in the general area of the Antarctic, and on the other, a number of Powers who, through their scientific expeditions and association with the Antarctic, can justifiably claim to participate in any arrangements which may be agreed upon to make a Treaty effective. The short answer to those who might ask why the drafting of a Treaty should be confined to 12 Powers would seem to be that a beginning must be made somewhere, and that the 12 are, by reason of their association in the Antarctic during the International Geophysical Year, well qualified to make that beginning. It was originally the view of the United Kingdom that some organisation vested with more effective and comprehensive powers than that which is now contemplated, would have been desirable, but in deference to the views of others we are prepared to subscribe to a less far-reaching scheme in the interests of general agreement. We feel, however, that the Treaty arrangements should be made as effective as possible, for if too many matters are left undecided they can give rise to subsequent disputes, which may prejudice the international harmony we are all anxious to promote. We therefore believe that the Treaty should include firm provisions for such matters as jurisdiction and the settlement of disputes between the parties. We should also regard the Treaty as unsatisfactory if it failed to set up some form of continuing organisation to promote its aims.

The other interlinked question is how to safeguard the interests of countries other than those represented at this Conference. We are concerned that no misunderstanding should arise as to the motives of the Twelve Powers; we should not wish our deliberations to raise doubts in the minds of other nations, and particularly of those who, although hitherto not actively interested in the Antarctic, may question the right of any single group of countries even to give the appearance of legislating on a matter of worldwide concern.

We believe, however, that a Treaty on the lines of that which is now proposed would provide a just and effective method of achieving the aim of preserving the Antarctic as a heritage from nature for the benefit of mankind in general, by freeing it as far as possible from the ambitions and disputes of nations and groups of nations. The Treaty is, in fact, to be almost entirely a self-denying ordinance on the part of the signatories, who will derive from it virtually no privileges but only obligations. In order to ensure the smooth working of the practical arrangements, which will give effect to the principles underlying the Treaty, it is desirable that these arrangements should be in the hands of those Powers having experience of physical conditions in the Antarctic. The Twelve Powers participating in this Conference have that experience, and it is surely reasonable that they should be charged, initially, with the responsibilities which will devolve upon them, as a consequence of the Treaty.

On the other hand, it is highly important in the interests of all nations—including those represented here—that any other country, which may wish to engage in activities in the Antarctic, should be able to associate itself with the terms of the Treaty and agree to abide by the principles which underly it. Insofar as these principles are in conformity with the spirit of the United Nations, we may hope that no member of the United Nations would decline to accept them, but there are various ways in which acceptance might be indicated, and this is a matter which, it seems to us, will merit further consideration by the delegates to this Conference. There is, I am sure, no need for other nations to fear that we shall fail to take their position into account, in the course of our discussions.

In conclusion, it is the belief of Her Majesty's Government in the United Kingdom that, if the principles which I have tried to outline can be accepted, it should be possible to devise a Treaty which will take fully into account the various and contrasting features, which are part of the picture: the need to preserve the legal position of the signatories; the need to protect the rights of non-signatories; the need for effectively preserving the Antarctic for peaceful uses; and, finally, the need to avoid anything which might unduly limit the activities of genuinely scientific expeditions. If we can forge an instrument which will maintain the balance between these considerations, I believe that we shall have made a very real contribution to the future, not only of the Antarctic, but also of the whole world. For here we have an opportunity to demonstrate the effectiveness of international cooperation, and if we are able, as a result of this Treaty, to transform an ideal into a reality, in a region which is admittedly remote and empty of people, may it not be, that the practice and the example which it will establish, will guide us towards a settlement of some of the graver problems which afflict the rest of the world, and to which we have so far failed to find a solution?

Conf. doc. 23, November 3, 1959

Statement by Mr. Daniels (*United States*)

Earlier this day you heard the general statement given by the Secretary of State which summarized the thinking of this Government in regard to the conference which is now convening. It gave our philosophy and summarized our objectives. Subsequently our Chairman, Ambassador Phleger, read our note of invitation which was addressed to all of your governments and which sets forth in more detail the thinking, the objectives, the policies of the United States Government. There is little that I need add to those statements at this time. I should be remiss in my duty, however, were I to let pass this occasion without expressing on behalf of the Delegation of the United States of America, our very sincere appreciation for the kind references which previous speakers have made to President Eisenhower, to the Secretary of State, and to our Chairman. I thank you all.

With reference to activities of countries in Antarctica over past years, it is not my intention to go into detail on that subject at this time. I have listened with interest and attention to the activities which many countries have pursued in Antarctica over past years. Were I to attempt to recount American activities over the past 140 years since the days of Captain Nathaniel Palmer of Connecticut, I would keep you here to an unseemly late hour and I shall refrain from doing so. I do wish, however, to make of record the fact that those activities have indeed been extensive and over a long period of time.

Having listened now to the eleven previous speakers it has become apparent that there does indeed exist wide areas of agreement among all of us in regard to the nature of the proposed treaty which we all hope will be concluded as a result of this conference. There is agreement—I think it has been expressed unanimously—with the proposition that Antarctica should be used for peaceful purposes only, and similarly there have been many good words in support of a continuation of the fruitful type of international scientific cooperation which has been going on there in recent years and which we hope can be continued indefinitely.

Other points have been mentioned and it has been quite apparent to me at least, and I hope to all of us, that indeed there is a very wide measure of agreement. That gives rise to a note of optimism and one on which I should like to conclude my brief statement today. That optimism is based not only on the substance of what previous speakers have said, but also on a recognition on our part of the very high caliber of statesmen which have been sent by eleven governments to participate in these debates. We are delighted to find with us distinguished gentlemen of such high caliber and I believe that that, combined with what I have just said, augurs well for the success of this Conference on Antarctica. It is our hope that not only will we conclude successfully a treaty along the general lines that have been outlined and which we will further refine, but also, having concluded that treaty, we hope that there will radiate forth from it and from Antarctica and into an otherwise troubled world, a little additional warmth of understanding, additional light and knowledge, and added hope for peace.

Conference Press Releases Nos. 1 to 5[1]

Press Release No. 1, October 16

The Conference, in its Second Plenary Session on October 16, adopted its Rules of Procedure and organized itself into two main committees, one of which [Committee II] will consider legal and political problems. The other committee [Committee I] will deal primarily with scientific matters.

Committee I held its first meeting during the afternoon.

Press Release No. 2, October 20

Committee II of the Conference on Antarctica, which is concerned with legal and political subjects, held its second committee meeting the afternoon of October 20. This Committee, the same as Committee I, consists of delegates representing all 12 countries participating in the Conference.

Following the practice of rotating chairmen, the Right Honorable Richard Gardiner Casey, C.H., Minister for External Affairs and head of the Australian delegation, presided.

In this committee session general agreement was reached that Antarctica should be used for peaceful purposes only and that all measures of a military nature should be prohibited.

It is anticipated this topic will become Article I of the treaty being negotiated.

Press Release No. 3, October 23

The Conference on Antarctica in which 12 nations are participating and which completed its seventh full working day Friday, October

---

[1] There were two other Conference press releases: press release No. 6, which summarized the main points contained in the treaty, was cancelled, and instead the full text of the treaty was made available to the press; press release No. 7, dated Nov. 30, announced that, agreement having been reached on the preamble and articles of the treaty and on the final act, final accord on the treaty as a whole would be considered at a plenary session on Dec. 1, to be followed by a signing ceremony.

23, announced that a spirit of cooperation prevails and that satisfactory progress is being made. During this period, the Conference has reached complete agreement on two topics. Numerous points involved in other topics of discussion have been agreed or clarified.

On October 20 it was announced that general agreement was reached that Antarctica should be used for peaceful purposes only and that all measures of a military nature should be prohibited.

General agreement has also been reached on international cooperation in scientific investigation in Antarctica. This topic is concerned with the exchange of information about plans for scientific programs, the exchange of scientific personnel between expeditions and stations, and the exchange of scientific observations and results.

During the seven working days there have been six Committee I meetings and five Committee II meetings. Committee I deals with scientific matters and Committee II with legal and political subjects.

Press Release No. 4, November 5

The Conference on Antarctica, approaching the end of three weeks of deliberations, has entered a new phase.

Committees I and II, having completed discussion of the items on their respective agendas, have been combined into a Committee of the Whole which is now considering the different positions expressed during the Committee meetings.

During the course of the Conference the Heads of Delegation have held a number of informal meetings to expedite discussions of substantive topics of the Treaty which is being negotiated.

Up to now there have been eleven Committee I and nine Committee II sessions. Committee I has concerned itself with scientific and technical subjects and Committee II with legal and political matters.

The following are among the topics which have been the subject of discussion at the Conference:

Preamble.
Use of Antarctica for peaceful purposes.
Freedom of scientific investigation in Antarctica.
International cooperation in scientific investigation in Antarctica.
Questions of rights and claims in Antarctica.
Observation and inspection for purposes of ensuring peaceful use and observance of the treaty's provisions.
Relationship of treaty to countries which are not parties.
Zone of application of the treaty.
Settlement of disputes arising under the treaty.

Provision for consultation.

Questions relating to jurisdiction in Antarctica.

Preliminary agreement has been reached on many of these items, subject to acceptance of the provisions as a whole.

It is hoped that by early next week the discussions will have proceeded to a point where there will be general agreement in principle between delegations, subject to final drafting and reference to governments.

Press Release No. 5, November 25

The Heads of Delegation met this morning to consider agreement on the remaining questions at issue. It had been hoped that it would be possible to reach final agreement this morning so a treaty could be signed on Friday.[1] However, owing to the failure to receive instructions, final agreement has not been possible. A further meeting of Heads of Delegation will be held at 10:30 a.m. Friday, at which time it is hoped that all representatives will have received their instructions.

---

[1] Nov. 27.

Final Plenary Session, December 1

(10:00–11:43 a.m.)

Mr. Phleger, Presiding

[EDITORIAL NOTE: Before the representatives made their concluding statements, the Chairman requested each delegation to indicate its formal approval of the text of the Treaty. Each representative in turn then signified his approval. The Conference thus unanimously adopted the Antarctic Treaty and opened it for signature.]

Conf. doc. 25, Annex A, December 1, 1959

Statement by Mr. Scilingo (*Argentina*)

On October 15, precisely one month and a half ago today, the sessions of the Antarctic Conference began, as a result of the initiative of one of the Parties in calling for such a conference on May 2, 1958.[1]

The list of topics was an arduous one and the objectives were, indeed, ambitious. Some of them called for decisions of principle and policy, which would come to bear upon some of the most serious contemporary problems. The Conference had before it a limited number of draft articles, which had been the object of discussions at sixty meetings of a working group made up of the representatives of the twelve participating countries. It had not yet been possible to reach common agreement on most of these.

During the inaugural session, the Heads of Delegations expressed a desire to reach agreement, thus overcoming obstacles arising from dissimilar positions and situations, with regard to a body of rules and formulae that might constitute a mutually satisfactory and unanimously acceptable Antarctic Treaty.

The document we are signing today, is the fruitful outcome of lengthy deliberations undertaken in an atmosphere of reciprocal good will, but it is, above all, the fruitful result of the foresight of the respective Governments, in response to something that, after all, was a challenge.

---

[1] See *ante*, pp. 2–4.

The Treaty establishes principles and precedents of historical significance. It neutralizes the Antarctic from the military standpoint, it forbids nuclear explosions and the disposal of radioactive waste throughout the whole area, it sets up a system of observation and control, and it provides for scientific research and cooperation together with the exchange of personnel and information, within a juridical framework that does not affect in any way the original positions of the Parties.

In one field, the nuclear one, the Treaty goes beyond the greatest expectations. The Argentine Delegation considers it as its duty to express its utmost satisfaction because of the significance of the decision and the spirit that inspired it.

Time will tell if the hopes that are based on the transcendental provisions of the Treaty are to be fully realized. Time will also tell whether the good examples they set forth, shall also achieve the desired results in broader fields of endeavor.

For the sake of Antarctica, to whose destiny and peaceful development it is indissolubly linked, and for the sake of the peace of the world, no other country wishes this to be so more ardently and tenaciously than the Argentine Republic.

Conf. doc. 25, Annex B, December 1, 1959

Statement by Mr. Beale (*Australia*)

Mr. Chairman, I should, first of all, like to congratulate you, Sir, upon the skilful, impartial, and courteous way in which you have presided over this Conference; also the Secretary General, Mr. Allen and his Secretariat for their faithful and assiduous labours. May I also compliment all delegates here upon the contributions which they each have made to our deliberations, and on the tolerance, goodwill and understanding which they have exhibited. This has been a fine Conference in which sincerity and the spirit of reasonableness have been abundantly manifest.

The Australian Government very gladly joins in this Treaty. Twelve nations, meeting in a spirit of genuine co-operation, have reached agreement upon four great principles. Firstly, that the vast Antarctic region shall be used only for peaceful purposes; there are to be no military measures in the Antarctic, and, to ensure this, there is to be complete mutual inspection throughout the area.

Secondly, that there shall be freedom of scientific investigation and full co-operation among all the parties to this Treaty, to the end that mankind's knowledge of this part of the earth may go forward for the benefit of present and future generations.

Thirdly, that the rights and claims to sovereignty of various parties shall not be renounced or prejudiced by the Treaty; nor shall the position be affected of those who may dispute such rights and claims.

Lastly we have reached agreement on the question of nuclear explosions in the Antarctic. The testing of nuclear weapons for military purposes is forbidden; and, pending general international agreement on the subject, non-military nuclear explosions also.

Mr. Chairman, let no man underestimate the importance of what has been done around this table. It is true that the Antarctic is a remote, lonely and inhospitable place with far more penguins on it than people; but it comprises a large part of this earth's surface; it is strategically important; and from its frozen wastes comes much of the weather of the nations of the Southern Hemisphere. Moreover, for all we know now, it may also be a great reservoir of raw materials capable some day of being exploited in the service of man. To have pledged the honour of all of the twelve nations present that this region shall remain free from international strife and rivalry and be the scene only of peaceful scientific and economic developments, is a major achievement. Such a document as this may well become a model for international agreements relating to other parts of this earth, and perhaps to the outer marches of space itself.

This is the belief which has carried us forward here, and we present this Treaty to the world confident that mankind will benefit greatly from it.

Conf. doc. 25, Annex C, December 1, 1959

Statement by Viscount Obert de Thieusies (*Belgium*)

Speaking in the name of the Belgian Delegation I would like to state the great satisfaction derived by us from our participation in the preparation of the Antarctic Treaty.

I have already had the opportunity on an earlier occasion to state the interest which always was and continues to be that of Belgium in the Antarctic Continent, and to say to what point my country is happy to be associated in an undertaking, the importance of which, we, like the other States represented here today, understand fully.

This Treaty will permit, or at least we hope so, to make that part of the world safe from any intrigue, whether military or otherwise. It will also make it possible for the various nations to carry on, in a spirit of sincere cooperation and mutual respect, the tasks of scientific research to which so many scientists from our various countries devoted their energies during the International Geophysical Year.

Belgium was happy to participate in this work, and will likewise be happy in the future to bring its share of effort to all the undertakings capable of contributing to the scientific and peaceful development of Antarctica. And if one day that Continent, which despite all efforts remains full of mystery, were to prove itself rich in unsuspected resources and capabilities, Belgium will consider it her duty to continue contributing in the undertakings of the other Nations interested in the development of Antarctica.

It is in such a spirit that we took part in the work of this Conference; it is in such a spirit that we will sign the Treaty which is the outcome of its deliberations, and it is in such a spirit that we will participate in the future in the meetings of the consultative committee the establishment of which is contemplated, and the duties of which are defined in Article IX of the Treaty.

Finally, I would like in my own name and in that of the other members of the Belgian Delegation to say how much we appreciated the friendly relations which we enjoyed with the members of the other delegations and of the Secretariat, and to express to our American hosts our deep gratitude for the hospitality extended to us.

Conf. doc. 25, Annex D, December 1, 1959

Statement by Mr. Mora (*Chile*)

With the signing of the Antarctic Treaty the bases have been laid down for a new system for the coexistence of nations separated geographically, with different political, social and economic systems, of different strength, and even of varied racial origins; but with similar purposes and interests within a Continent of exceptional characteristics.

It has not been easy to reach this agreement, because not all of us meeting here had disciplined our spirits to the management of ideas such as that of freedom of scientific research, as that of a controlled peace, that of the prohibition of tests of weapons of war, and of nuclear explosions, that of the freezing of rights, in a formula that without impairing neither titles nor sovereignties, guards against all danger that a tranquil coexistence might be disturbed.

Someone said, during a debate, that we were drafting a document that could mean the beginning of a new era for the world. And, doubtless, it must be so if good will and reciprocal trust contribute to faithful compliance with the common principles that we have here codified.

Given such a noble example, we may see all the peoples of mankind at a time not too far off, enjoying as in the Antarctic, the results of a cooperation fruitful in accomplishment for the common good, of an enduring peace that lifts from the heart of man distrust and fear, and of the permanent enjoyment of loyal friendship that will permit the solution of all differences without discord.

Chile places its signature to this Antarctic Treaty with lofty intentions and with full confidence that all the obligations hereby undertaken of collaboration, of reciprocity, of peace, of mutual respect for the rights of each other, and of progress and general welfare, will be complied with in the degree necessary so that none of the noble inspirations we have pursued here so tenaciously, will be frustrated.

If it turns out this way, then we would have the satisfaction of seeing the Antarctic converted into a better region than the rest of the world, and into a precedent worthy of imitation.

Conf. doc. 25, Annex E, December 1, 1959

Statement by Mr. Charpentier (*France*)

The care with which the French Government followed the work of the Conference on Antarctica reflects the interest that it attached to the success of our negotiations. The Treaty which we are about to sign will make it possible for scientists of all countries to carry on, in the harsh climate of the South Pole, the task undertaken during the International Geophysical Year and to probe into the mysteries which Nature defends so fiercely in the South Polar Continent.

As we look back, we can justly feel that it is an exceptional success to have been able to conquer so many obstacles which, to us, seemed as insurmountable as those with which the daring explorers of Antarctica had to cope. We had so many interests and such serious political problems to take into consideration; we had to be careful not to arouse the fears that any one of us could come to feel, and to reconcile our decisions with the actual facts of the internal or the foreign policy of our own country. Each day that went by could bring about the failure of the Conference, but each day that passed brought to us a strengthened hope of success. And it is with the thought that we were all working for the peace and welfare of mankind that we persevered in the task before us, that we avoided clashes, that we succeeded in sparing the feelings of the parties involved and that we finally succeeded in concluding the Treaty in [*on*] Antarctica.

For nearly one hundred and twenty years France has been present in Adélie Land, over which it has sovereignty and the Government of the Republic, to the extent to which its indefeasible rights are respected, is determined to do its part in the peaceful task that will be undertaken in Antarctica by scientists and research workers, in accordance with the Treaty.

The fact that the Treaty prohibits any military installation and activity in the South Polar Continent and that it is in full consonance with the efforts of mankind to solve the problems relating to the maintenance of peace in the world, is most gratifying to my country. In order to ensure the observance of the non-militarization in Antarctica the French Government, bearing in mind the particular conditions prevailing in this area, has accepted that simplified forms of inspection be applied for the time being. These latter, in its opinion, must some day be replaced by a genuine international control within the framework of a world disarmament organization, which it is our hope will soon come into being.

The French delegation has particularly appreciated the spirit of mutual understanding, goodwill and, I shall even say friendship, in which our negotiations were held. Our success is a good omen on the eve of the important meeting on which rest the hopes of mankind.

May I be permitted in concluding to express the gratitude of the French Government for the Statesman who is at the origin of our success, since it is upon his invitation that this Conference was held. May I be allowed to extend my thanks to President Eisenhower and the Government of the United States for the excellent organization of our work and for the cordial welcome we received in Washington.

Conf. doc. 25, Annex F, December 1, 1959

Statement by Mr. Asakai (*Japan*)

We are gratified to be here to affix our signatures to the Antarctic Treaty.

We have met for the past six weeks and have succeeded in establishing the principles of peaceful use of Antarctica and freedom of scientific research there. It is virtually unprecedented to provide for non-militarization with inspection in such a vast expanse as that of Antarctica. In view of the great strategic potential there, this would be a bold and welcome step towards the promotion of world peace.

Underlying these principles, Mr. Chairman, is the legal formula we have so carefully worked out whereby opposing positions of claimant and non-claimant countries are frozen in connection with territorial rights on Antarctica. It is on this firm legal foundation that all parties have been able to agree to such advanced and progressive measures as non-militarization, inspection to that end, the control of nuclear explosions and freedom of scientific research there.

Our as yet unexplored Antarctica has boundless potentialities. So has our new Treaty. Politically, legally and scientifically the importance of this Treaty is inestimable; its future is bright with promise. How bright that future actually becomes, however, depends upon our faithfulness and sincerity. No matter how flawless a treaty may be, the participating countries must implement and promote the purposes and principles of that treaty in practice, or it fails. You may be sure, Mr. Chairman, that the Government and people of Japan will abide by the provisions of our Treaty in good faith and with good grace.

Conf. doc. 25, Annex G, December 1, 1959

Statement by Mr. White (*New Zealand*)

We have completed our work and are agreed on the terms of the Antarctic Treaty.

The twelve nations represented here are clearly entitled to take pride in what they have accomplished. My Prime Minister, the Right Honourable Walter Nash, who led the New Zealand delegation during the earlier stages of the negotiations, has asked me to convey to the Conference his keen personal satisfaction at the successful conclusion of the Treaty.

The Treaty we are signing today will ensure that Antarctica will forever remain an area of peace, free from war and warlike preparations, shielded against political rivalries and devoted to pursuits which will be of benefit to all mankind.

We have just recently been reminded that the enlargement of our knowledge about Antarctica, even in today's conditions, has its own hardships and dangers. A few weeks ago, during the course of this Conference, a tractor carrying three New Zealanders fell down a hidden crevasse in Antarctica. One man was killed and two were badly injured. A United States party in the area lent valuable assistance in rescuing the injured. These men were on scientific expeditions and were risking their lives, as many other brave men have done before in Antarctica, in seeking to add to what is known about the southern continent.

It has always been the New Zealand view that scientific activity in Antarctica should be carried out in future, as it has been in the past, in peaceful conditions, by cooperative means, and for the benefit of all. The present Treaty will assure these objectives. The New Zealand Government therefore believes its conclusion to be a step of the greatest significance.

New Zealand is geographically close to Antarctica. New Zealand has a lengthy record of Antarctic achievement. We have asserted our claim to sovereignty. We have conducted exploration and scientific research both in our own right and in cooperation with other countries, for example in the epic trans-Antarctic expedition of 1957, in the International Geophysical Year, and in programmes of mutual assistance to American expeditions at present operating in Antarctica.

However, we look towards future cooperation with other countries also. The Treaty provides for the accession of additional countries who may wish to subscribe to its objectives. It does not endeavor to set up a monopolistic regime for the original twelve signatory parties.

We believe that this Treaty conforms with the principles and purposes of the United Nations Charter. Provision has also been made to bring it into consonance with future international agreements concerning, for example, the uses of fissionable material. The testing of nuclear weapons is to be prohibited completely in Antarctica and the peaceful use of nuclear explosions for scientific or developmental purposes is to be deferred until a more far-reaching international agreement can be concluded ensuring the safety of such activity.

The negotiation of this Treaty has not been a simple task. We have had to overcome many difficulties of detail in drafting a precise text. We have worked intensively for many weeks, even after allowing for months of preparatory work extending back to early 1958. But we have never lost sight of our major objectives. Therefore today we can be justifiably proud of our achievement and can confidently commend the Antarctic Treaty for the approval of the rest of the world.

In doing so we are encouraged to hope that the spirit which has animated the conclusion of this Treaty will prevail in other areas of international negotiation.

Conf. doc. 25, Annex H, December 1, 1959

Statement by Mr. Koht (*Norway*)

I would like to join with those who have spoken before me in expressing the satisfaction of my Government with the results achieved at this Conference.

We set out to guarantee that a vast continent should be used for peaceful purposes only and that there should be freedom of scientific investigation and international scientific cooperation in Antarctica. Like all members of expeditions into uncharted territory we have had to go through periods of adjustment, and my Government, in the same way as others represented here, has had to accept certain provisions that it would have preferred to be different. I think, however, it may safely be said that the Conference never lost sight of its goal, and that we did reach it. I shall therefore be most happy to recommend to my Government that the Treaty be ratified in accordance with the Norwegian Constitution.

The thrilling saga of Antarctica has inspired men everywhere with its emphasis on basic human values—courage, patience and willingness to work together towards a common goal. I hope that the chapter which we have added here, will not be found to be entirely void of these values, and that it may inspire men to undertake similar ventures to promote peace and international cooperation in other fields.

I cannot conclude these remarks without expressing my deep-felt gratitude to the Government of the United States for its hospitality, to you Mr. Chairman for your distinguished and always tactful conduct of our negotiations, and to the Secretary General and his able staff for courteous and efficient service.

Conf. doc. 25, Annex I, December 1, 1959

Statement by Mr. du Plessis (*Union of South Africa*)

Mr. Chairman, nearly seven weeks have passed since we commenced our deliberations on the Treaty we are about to sign. These deliberations have been marked by frank exchanges of views and opinions and it is a tribute to the refreshing spirit of enquiry and of cooperation, and where necessary of compromise, displayed by my colleagues, the Heads of the various national delegations, that these negotiations have been carried to so successful a conclusion. We are all conscious of our debt to you, Sir, for successfully guiding us through the intricacies of negotiation. Both as Conference Chairman and as Chairman of the meetings of Heads of Delegations your wisdom, your understanding and your example have been an encouragement to all of us who have laboured for what we believed to be necessary and equitable arrangements governing our relations in Antarctica. The Secretary-General and his staff have worked hard and diligently to keep the Conference arrangements on a smooth and even course. We extend sincere thanks also to them.

In so far as the Treaty itself is concerned I need not, I trust, emphasise the great importance which my country attaches to the principles of non-militarization and of international scientific cooperation for peaceful purposes which are enshrined in it. As a country whose nearest overseas neighbour is precisely the continent of Antarctica, the Union of South Africa and indeed all of Southern Africa, cannot but have a high sense of appreciation for what has been achieved at this Conference.

It is comforting to know that our national Antarctic expedition which sailed from Cape Town for the remote South a few days ago, will have commenced its odyssey at almost the precise moment that this Treaty ushers in what we all, I am sure, hope will be an enduring era of peaceful cooperation in Antarctica, from which not only the nations whose representatives are gathered around this table, but all mankind, must profit.

For the first time in history the opportunity has been created for one of the continents of this world, admittedly the most barren and desolate one, to be freed from the threat of destructive war. It is my hope that this beginning will not only be a contribution to the relaxation of tensions and to the breaking down of the cold war but that it might establish a pattern also in other spheres of international life through which universal understanding and cooperation might be ushered in. If the olive branch of peace has to be carried into the world from the barren wastes of Antarctica then, paradoxical as it may seem, it is as good a starting place as any for so momentous a mission.

Conf. doc. 25, Annex J, December 1, 1959

Statement by Mr. Kuznetsov (*Soviet Union*)

The Conference on Antarctica is ending its work today. The Conference proceeded in an atmosphere of business-like cooperation and mutual understanding which yielded fruitful results. An international treaty on Antarctica has been worked out.

The treaty stipulates that Antarctica may be used for peaceful purposes only, that no measures of a military nature, including the establishment of military bases and fortifications, the carrying out of military maneuvers and the testing of any type of weapons may be undertaken in this area.

Agreement has also been reached on the prohibition of any nuclear explosion in Antarctica and of the disposal of radioactive materials in this area.

These treaty provisions serve the main objective now facing mankind, namely, to preserve and strengthen peace among all nations. At the same time they open broad prospects for the development of cooperation between states in the exploration of Antarctica.

The principle of scientific investigation in Antarctica is an important provision of the treaty. This principle, universally recognized during the International Geophysical Year, means that governments, organizations and citizens of all countries may carry out scientific investigations in Antarctica on an equal basis, which will undoubtedly promote a more effective exploration of this area.

Fruitful international scientific cooperation in Antarctica will be promoted by the confirmation and further development in the treaty of the established specific forms of cooperation between scientists of different countries, including reciprocal exchange of scientific personnel. Joint efforts of scientists from as many countries as possible, wide exchange of results of observations, and close contacts between expeditions in Antarctica will permit sooner the revelation of the secrets of the Antarctic Continent, which have so far been insufficiently explored.

The achievement of agreement on such a complicated and delicate problem as territorial claims in Antarctica was the result of efforts to cooperate on the part of all participants in the Conference. The treaty provides that the positions of signatory States shall not be impaired in this respect. Such a solution should contribute to the situation where the possibility of conflicts arising between states in Antarctica would be prevented.

The Conference has successfully resolved the question of the adoption of measures to enforce the treaty, which include the establishment of an inspection system, a consultative procedure for the solution of operational problems, etc.

There is every reason to believe that the treaty as worked out by the Conference will be an important contribution to the cause of further development of scientific cooperation in Antarctica and will promote confidence between states. The Conference on Antarctica is an additional evidence of the fact that states, if they are ready to cooperate, can successfully achieve through negotiations mutually acceptable solutions of international problems in the interest of universal peace and progress.

Both the Conference and the treaty on Antarctica reflect a definite improvement in international situations and constitute in themselves a positive contribution to the cause of further development of mutual understanding between states.

On behalf of the Soviet Delegation I congratulate all participants in the Conference on Antarctica upon its successful termination.

Allow me also to express our gratitude to the Government of the United States of America for its hospitality and for providing the facilities necessary for the work of the Conference.

Conf. doc. 25, Annex K, December 1, 1959

Statement by Sir Harold Caccia (*United Kingdom*)

In his statement at the opening plenary Session of the Conference, Sir Esler Dening, speaking as leader of the United Kingdom Delegation, pointed out that Her Majesty's Government in the United Kingdom had for many years been in favour of the conclusion of an agreement between the countries actively interested in the Antarctic. He also expressed the hope that the Conference would be able to devise a Treaty which would take fully into account the interests of all the powers concerned, or likely to be concerned, with the area. I think that we can fairly say that that object has been achieved.

No Treaty of course ever gives complete satisfaction to all its signatories. We in the United Kingdom Delegation fully realise that others have made concessions in the interest of mutual agreement just as we have ourselves. It is because of the conciliatory spirit that has been displayed throughout the Conference that we are now about to sign the Antarctic Treaty.

The International Geophysical Year showed what could be achieved by international co-operation in scientific research in the Antarctic. It is our belief that the present Treaty will serve as a firm framework within which co-operation will continue in the scientific field and be extended to others.

We also attach great importance to the requirement that the Antarctic shall be used for peaceful purposes only and to the provisions designed to ensure that friendly international relations shall not be disturbed by political disputes arising from the area. The Treaty is, of course, not merely a statement of principles; it also contains provisions, appropriate to the special conditions in the Antarctic, to ensure that its terms are observed in practice.

I need hardly remind you that the principles on which the Treaty is based are those set out in President Eisenhower's original invitation. I should like to take this opportunity to pay tribute to the United States Government for the part which they have played in making this Treaty a reality. I also wish, on behalf of the United Kingdom Delegation, to thank the United States Government for making available to the Conference the Secretariat who have served us so well.

The problems of this remote and unpeopled region might be thought to be of little relevance to the great issues that concern the world to-day. But they are problems to which the 12 nations represented here have attached importance and which have created real difficulties for some of them. It is our hope that the successful conclusion of this Treaty will be a good omen and will contribute to the establishment of a climate more favourable to the settlement of other international questions. In that case, the Treaty will have had an importance far transcending the Antarctic.

Conf. doc. 25, Annex L, December 1, 1959

Statement by Mr. Daniels (*United States*)

Today we have brought to successful conclusion our joint efforts to conclude the first treaty covering the vast expanse of Antarctica. All of us will long remember this historic occasion. Furthermore, the conclusion of this unusual and unprecedented treaty will be deeply engraved in the annals of history.

This is no treaty of selfish monopoly. This treaty is not of a monopolistic or colonialistic character. It is neither land-grabbing nor land-dividing. Rather, it is aimed at achieving rational and constructive solutions in Antarctica. This treaty is of a broad and generous character. The significance of its three major objectives is readily apparent:

1. We have agreed that Antarctica shall be used for peaceful purposes only. In the world today peace, like war, tends to become indivisible. Accordingly, in reaching this solemn agreement among ourselves, we have thereby contributed to the establishment of peace in the world at large. This is of advantage to peoples everywhere.

2. We have agreed that there shall be freedom of scientific cooperation in Antarctica and international cooperation to that end. The beneficial results of this international scientific cooperation will be enjoyed by all of the countries participating in it. Even more, since science has a tendency to surmount nationalistic barriers, the contributions we make to science in Antarctica, by making it freely available, will be of obvious benefit to all countries and contribute to the enlightenment of man.

3. A third major objective has been successfully achieved, namely, the prohibition on all nuclear explosions in Antarctica for the purpose of preventing radioactive fallout. This achievement, in which we have all agreed today, is of obvious benefit to all regions in the world, and not solely to those of us which have signed this solemn agreement. The little speck of radioactive dust drifting in the upper air does not know when it comes to earth whether it will light on a section of the map colored black or white or brown or yellow or red. Certainly we do not wish it to fall on our lands; nor do we wish it to fall on anybody else's land.

In these three major ways we have concluded basic agreements which will be of benefit to ourselves, and of benefit to all mankind. It is in that spirit that the United States has been proud to associate itself with the other countries represented at this Conference in concluding these broad and far-reaching agreements on Antarctica.

Final Act of the Conference on Antarctica, December 1[1]

Conf. doc. 27, December 1, 1959

The Governments of Argentina, Australia, Belgium, Chile, the French Republic, Japan, New Zealand, Norway, the Union of South Africa, the Union of Soviet Socialist Republics, the United Kingdom of Great Britain and Northern Ireland, and the United States of America,

Having accepted the invitation extended to them on May 2, 1958,[2] by the Government of the United States of America to participate in a Conference on Antarctica to be attended by representatives of the twelve nations which cooperated in the Antarctic Program of the International Geophysical Year;

Appointed their respective Representatives, who are listed below by countries:

ARGENTINA

Representative

His Excellency
Adolfo Scilingo
(*Head of Delegation*)

Alternate Representative

Dr. Francisco R. Bello

AUSTRALIA

Representatives

The Right Honorable
Richard Gardiner Casey, C.H., D.S.O., M.C., M.P.
(*Head of Delegation*)

His Excellency the Honorable
Howard Beale, Q.C.
(*Deputy Head of Delegation*)

---

[1] Signed by the appropriate members of each delegation at the fourth and final plenary session of the Conference on Dec. 1, 1959.

[2] See *ante*, pp. 2–4.

Alternate Representatives
>J. C. G. Kevin
>
>M. R. Booker

BELGIUM

Representative
>His Excellency
>Viscount Obert de Thieusies
>(*Head of Delegation*)

Alternate Representatives
>Jean de Bassompierre
>Alfred van der Essen

CHILE

Representatives
>His Excellency
>Marcial Mora
>(*Head of Delegation*)
>His Excellency
>Enrique Gajardo
>His Excellency
>Julio Escudero

Alternate Representative
>Horacio Suárez

THE FRENCH REPUBLIC

Representative
>His Excellency
>Pierre Charpentier
>(*Head of Delegation*)

Alternate Representative
>Guy Scalabre

JAPAN

Representatives
>His Excellency
>Koichiro Asakai
>(*Head of Delegation*)
>Takeso Shimoda

NEW ZEALAND

Representatives
>The Right Honorable
>Walter Nash, C.H.
>(*Head of Delegation*)
>A. D. McIntosh, C.M.G.
>(*Deputy Head of Delegation*)

Alternate Representative
>G. D. L. White, M.V.O.

Representatives

His Excellency
Paul Koht
(*Head of Delegation*)

Torfinn Oftedal
(*Deputy Head of Delegation*)

Alternate Representatives

Dr. Anders K. Orvin

Gunnar Haerum

UNION OF SOUTH AFRICA

Representatives

The Honorable
Eric H. Louw
(*Head of Delegation*)

His Excellency
W. C. du Plessis
(*Deputy Head of Delegation*)

Alternate Representatives

J. G. Stewart

A. G. Dunn

D. Stuart Franklin

UNION OF SOVIET SOCIALIST REPUBLICS

Representatives

His Excellency
Vasili V. Kuznetsov
(*Head of Delegation*)

Grigory I. Tunkin

Alternate Representatives

Alexander A. Afanasiev

Vice Admiral Valentin A. Chekurov

Mikhail M. Somov

Mikhail N. Smirnovsky

UNITED KINGDOM OF GREAT BRITAIN AND NORTHERN IRELAND

Representatives

Sir Esler Dening, G.C.M.G., O.B.E.
(*Head of Delegation*)

His Excellency
Sir Harold Caccia, G.C.M.G., K.C.V.O.

Alternate Representatives

H. N. Brain, C.M.G., O.B.E.

The Viscount Hood, C.M.G.

The Honorable
H. A. A. Hankey, C.V.O.

UNITED STATES OF AMERICA

Representative

The Honorable Herman Phleger
(*Head of Delegation*)

Alternate Representatives

The Honorable Paul C. Daniels
George H. Owen

The Conference met at Washington on October 15, 1959. It had before it as a basis for discussion working papers considered in the course of informal preparatory talks among representatives of the twelve countries who had met in Washington following the aforesaid invitation of the Government of the United States of America.

At the opening Plenary Session of the Conference the Honorable Herman Phleger, Head of the United States Delegation, was elected Chairman of the Conference. Mr. Henry E. Allen was appointed Secretary General of the Conference and Rapporteur.

The Conference established two Committees under rotating chairmanship to deal with the items on the agenda of the Conference. Following initial consideration of such items, these Committees were reconstituted as a Committee of the Whole. There were also established a Credentials Committee, a Drafting Committee, and a Committee on Style.

The final session of the Conference was held on December 1, 1959.

As a result of the deliberations of the Conference, as recorded in the summary records and reports of the respective Committees and of the Plenary Sessions, the Conference formulated and submitted for signature on December 1, 1959, the Antarctic Treaty.

The Conference recommended to the participating Governments that they appoint representatives to meet in Washington within two months after the signing of the Treaty and thereafter at such times as may be convenient, pending the entry into force of the Treaty, to consult together and to recommend to their Governments such interim arrangements regarding the matters dealt with in the Treaty as they may deem desirable.[1]

IN WITNESS WHEREOF, the following Plenipotentiaries sign this Final Act.

DONE at Washington this first day of December, one thousand nine hundred and fifty-nine, in the English, French, Russian and Spanish languages, each version being equally authentic, in a single original which shall be deposited in the archives of the Government of the

---

[1] Representatives of the signatories held the first of several meetings on Jan. 27, 1960.

United States of America. The Government of the United States of America shall transmit certified copies thereof to all the other Governments represented at the Conference.

[Here follow the French, Russian, and Spanish texts.]

FOR ARGENTINA: ADOLFO SCILINGO
                                                  F. R. BELLO

FOR AUSTRALIA: HOWARD BEALE
                                                  J. C. G. KEVIN
                                                  M. R. BOOKER

FOR BELGIUM: OBERT DE THIEUSIES

FOR CHILE: MARCIAL MORA
                                                  E. GAJARDO
                                                  JULIO ESCUDERO

FOR THE FRENCH REPUBLIC: PIERRE CHARPENTIER
                                                  G. SCALABRE

FOR JAPAN: KOICHIRO ASAKAI
                                                  T. SHIMODA

FOR NEW ZEALAND: G. D. L. WHITE

FOR NORWAY: PAUL KOHT

FOR THE UNION OF SOUTH AFRICA: WENTZEL C. DU PLESSIS

FOR THE UNION OF SOVIET
   SOCIALIST REPUBLICS: В. Кузнецов [1]
                                                  Г. Тункин [2]

FOR THE UNITED KINGDOM OF GREAT
   BRITAIN AND NORTHERN IRELAND: HAROLD CACCIA

FOR THE UNITED STATES OF AMERICA: HERMAN PHLEGER
                                                  PAUL C. DANIELS

---

[1] V. Kuznetsov.
[2] G. Tunkin.

60

The Antarctic Treaty, December 1[1]

Conf. doc. 28, December 1, 1959

The Governments of Argentina, Australia, Belgium, Chile, the French Republic, Japan, New Zealand, Norway, the Union of South Africa, the Union of Soviet Socialist Republics, the United Kingdom of Great Britain and Northern Ireland, and the United States of America,

Recognizing that it is in the interest of all mankind that Antarctica shall continue forever to be used exclusively for peaceful purposes and shall not become the scene or object of international discord;

Acknowledging the substantial contributions to scientific knowledge resulting from international cooperation in scientific investigation in Antarctica;

Convinced that the establishment of a firm foundation for the continuation and development of such cooperation on the basis of freedom of scientific investigation in Antarctica as applied during the International Geophysical Year accords with the interests of science and the progress of all mankind;

Convinced also that a treaty ensuring the use of Antarctica for peaceful purposes only and the continuance of international harmony in Antarctica will further the purposes and principles embodied in the Charter of the United Nations;

Have agreed as follows:

ARTICLE I

1. Antarctica shall be used for peaceful purposes only. There shall be prohibited, *inter alia*, any measures of a military nature, such as the establishment of military bases and fortifications, the carrying out of military maneuvers, as well as the testing of any type of weapons.

2. The present Treaty shall not prevent the use of military personnel or equipment for scientific research or for any other peaceful purpose.

ARTICLE II

Freedom of scientific investigation in Antarctica and cooperation toward that end, as applied during the International Geophysical Year, shall continue, subject to the provisions of the present Treaty.

---

[1] Signed by the duly authorized representatives at a special ceremony following the fourth and final plenary session of the Conference on Dec. 1, 1959.

Article III

1. In order to promote international cooperation in scientific investigation in Antarctica, as provided for in Article II of the present Treaty, the Contracting Parties agree that, to the greatest extent feasible and practicable:

(a) information regarding plans for scientific programs in Antarctica shall be exchanged to permit maximum economy and efficiency of operations;

(b) scientific personnel shall be exchanged in Antarctica between expeditions and stations;

(c) scientific observations and results from Antarctica shall be exchanged and made freely available.

2. In implementing this Article, every encouragement shall be given to the establishment of cooperative working relations with those Specialized Agencies of the United Nations and other international organizations having a scientific or technical interest in Antarctica.

Article IV

1. Nothing contained in the present Treaty shall be interpreted as:

(a) a renunciation by any Contracting Party of previously asserted rights of or claims to territorial sovereignty in Antarctica;

(b) a renunciation or diminution by any Contracting Party of any basis of claim to territorial sovereignty in Antarctica which it may have whether as a result of its activities or those of its nationals in Antarctica, or otherwise;

(c) prejudicing the position of any Contracting Party as regards its recognition or non-recognition of any other State's right of or claim or basis of claim to territorial sovereignty in Antarctica.

2. No acts or activities taking place while the present Treaty is in force shall constitute a basis for asserting, supporting or denying a claim to territorial sovereignty in Antarctica or create any rights of sovereignty in Antarctica. No new claim, or enlargement of an existing claim, to territorial sovereignty in Antarctica shall be asserted while the present Treaty is in force.

Article V

1. Any nuclear explosions in Antarctica and the disposal there of radioactive waste material shall be prohibited.

2. In the event of the conclusion of international agreements concerning the use of nuclear energy, including nuclear explosions and the disposal of radioactive waste material, to which all of the Contracting Parties whose representatives are entitled to participate in the

meetings provided for under Article IX are parties, the rules established under such agreements shall apply in Antarctica.

ARTICLE VI

The provisions of the present Treaty shall apply to the area south of 60° South Latitude, including all ice shelves, but nothing in the present Treaty shall prejudice or in any way affect the rights, or the exercise of the rights, of any State under international law with regard to the high seas within that area.

ARTICLE VII

1. In order to promote the objectives and ensure the observance of the provisions of the present Treaty, each Contracting Party whose representatives are entitled to participate in the meetings referred to in Article IX of the Treaty shall have the right to designate observers to carry out any inspection provided for by the present Article. Observers shall be nationals of the Contracting Parties which designate them. The names of observers shall be communicated to every other Contracting Party having the right to designate observers, and like notice shall be given of the termination of their appointment.

2. Each observer designated in accordance with the provisions of paragraph 1 of this Article shall have complete freedom of access at any time to any or all areas of Antarctica.

3. All areas of Antarctica, including all stations, installations and equipment within those areas, and all ships and aircraft at points of discharging or embarking cargoes or personnel in Antarctica, shall be open at all times to inspection by any observers designated in accordance with paragraph 1 of this Article.

4. Aerial observation may be carried out at any time over any or all areas of Antarctica by any of the Contracting Parties having the right to designate observers.

5. Each Contracting Party shall, at the time when the present Treaty enters into force for it, inform the other Contracting Parties, and thereafter shall give them notice in advance, of

(a) all expeditions to and within Antarctica, on the part of its ships or nationals, and all expeditions to Antarctica organized in or proceeding from its territory;

(b) all stations in Antarctica occupied by its nationals; and

(c) any military personnel or equipment intended to be introduced by it into Antarctica subject to the conditions prescribed in paragraph 2 of Article I of the present Treaty.

Article VIII

1. In order to facilitate the exercise of their functions under the present Treaty, and without prejudice to the respective positions of the Contracting Parties relating to jurisdiction over all other persons in Antarctica, observers designated under paragraph 1 of Article VII and scientific personnel exchanged under subparagraph 1(b) of Article III of the Treaty, and members of the staffs accompanying any such persons, shall be subject only to the jurisdiction of the Contracting Party of which they are nationals in respect of all acts or omissions occurring while they are in Antarctica for the purpose of exercising their functions.

2. Without prejudice to the provisions of paragraph 1 of this Article, and pending the adoption of measures in pursuance of subparagraph 1(e) of Article IX, the Contracting Parties concerned in any case of dispute with regard to the exercise of jurisdiction in Antarctica shall immediately consult together with a view to reaching a mutually acceptable solution.

Article IX

1. Representatives of the Contracting Parties named in the preamble to the present Treaty shall meet at the City of Canberra within two months after the date of entry into force of the Treaty, and thereafter at suitable intervals and places, for the purpose of exchanging information, consulting together on matters of common interest pertaining to Antarctica, and formulating and considering, and recommending to their Governments, measures in furtherance of the principles and objectives of the Treaty, including measures regarding:

(a) use of Antarctica for peaceful purposes only;

(b) facilitation of scientific research in Antarctica;

(c) facilitation of international scientific cooperation in Antarctica;

(d) facilitation of the exercise of the rights of inspection provided for in Article VII of the Treaty;

(e) questions relating to the exercise of jurisdiction in Antarctica;

(f) preservation and conservation of living resources in Antarctica.

2. Each Contracting Party which has become a party to the present Treaty by accession under Article XIII shall be entitled to appoint representatives to participate in the meetings referred to in paragraph 1 of the present Article, during such time as that Contracting Party demonstrates its interest in Antarctica by conducting substantial scientific research activity there, such as the establishment of a scientific station or the despatch of a scientific expedition.

3. Reports from the observers referred to in Article VII of the present Treaty shall be transmitted to the representatives of the Contracting Parties participating in the meetings referred to in paragraph 1 of the present Article.

4. The measures referred to in paragraph 1 of this Article shall become effective when approved by all the Contracting Parties whose representatives were entitled to participate in the meetings held to consider those measures.

5. Any or all of the rights established in the present Treaty may be exercised as from the date of entry into force of the Treaty whether or not any measures facilitating the exercise of such rights have been proposed, considered or approved as provided in this Article.

Article X

Each of the Contracting Parties undertakes to exert appropriate efforts, consistent with the Charter of the United Nations, to the end that no one engages in any activity in Antarctica contrary to the principles or purposes of the present Treaty.

Article XI

1. If any dispute arises between two or more of the Contracting Parties concerning the interpretation or application of the present Treaty, those Contracting Parties shall consult among themselves with a view to having the dispute resolved by negotiation, inquiry, mediation, conciliation, arbitration, judicial settlement or other peaceful means of their own choice.

2. Any dispute of this character not so resolved shall, with the consent, in each case, of all parties to the dispute, be referred to the International Court of Justice for settlement; but failure to reach agreement on reference to the International Court shall not absolve parties to the dispute from the responsibility of continuing to seek to resolve it by any of the various peaceful means referred to in paragraph 1 of this Article.

Article XII

1. (a) The present Treaty may be modified or amended at any time by unanimous agreement of the Contracting Parties whose representatives are entitled to participate in the meetings provided for under Article IX. Any such modification or amendment shall enter into force when the depositary Government has received notice from all such Contracting Parties that they have ratified it.

(b) Such modification or amendment shall thereafter enter into force as to any other Contracting Party when notice of ratification by it has been received by the depositary Government. Any such Contracting Party from which no notice of ratification is received within a period of two years from the date of entry into force of the modification or amendment in accordance with the provisions of subparagraph 1(a) of this Article shall be deemed to have withdrawn from the present Treaty on the date of the expiration of such period.

2. (a) If after the expiration of thirty years from the date of entry into force of the present Treaty, any of the Contracting Parties whose representatives are entitled to participate in the meetings provided for under Article IX so requests by a communication addressed to the depositary Government, a Conference of all the Contracting Parties shall be held as soon as practicable to review the operation of the Treaty.

(b) Any modification or amendment to the present Treaty which is approved at such a Conference by a majority of the Contracting Parties there represented, including a majority of those whose representatives are entitled to participate in the meetings provided for under Article IX, shall be communicated by the depositary Government to all the Contracting Parties immediately after the termination of the Conference and shall enter into force in accordance with the provisions of paragraph 1 of the present Article.

(c) If any such modification or amendment has not entered into force in accordance with the provisions of subparagraph 1(a) of this Article within a period of two years after the date of its communication to all the Contracting Parties, any Contracting Party may at any time after the expiration of that period give notice to the depositary Government of its withdrawal from the present Treaty; and such withdrawal shall take effect two years after the receipt of the notice by the depositary Government.

ARTICLE XIII

1. The present Treaty shall be subject to ratification by the signatory States. It shall be open for accession by any State which is a Member of the United Nations, or by any other State which may be invited to accede to the Treaty with the consent of all the Contracting Parties whose representatives are entitled to participate in the meetings provided for under Article IX of the Treaty.

2. Ratification of or accession to the present Treaty shall be effected by each State in accordance with its constitutional processes.

3. Instruments of ratification and instruments of accession shall be deposited with the Government of the United States of America, hereby designated as the depositary Government.

4. The depositary Government shall inform all signatory and acceding States of the date of each deposit of an instrument of ratification or accession, and the date of entry into force of the Treaty and of any modification or amendment thereto.

5. Upon the deposit of instruments of ratification by all the signatory States, the present Treaty shall enter into force for those States and for States which have deposited instruments of accession. Thereafter the Treaty shall enter into force for any acceding State upon the deposit of its instrument of accession.

6. The present Treaty shall be registered by the depositary Government pursuant to Article 102 of the Charter of the United Nations.

ARTICLE XIV

The present Treaty, done in the English, French, Russian and Spanish languages, each version being equally authentic, shall be deposited in the archives of the Government of the United States of America, which shall transmit duly certified copies thereof to the Governments of the signatory and acceding States.

[Here follow the French, Russian, and Spanish texts of the foregoing.]

IN WITNESS WHEREOF, the undersigned Plenipotentiaries, duly authorized, have signed the present Treaty.

DONE at Washington this first day of December, one thousand nine hundred and fifty-nine.

[Here follow the French, Russian, and Spanish texts of the testimonial paragraphs.]

FOR ARGENTINA:	ADOLFO SCILINGO
	F. R. BELLO
FOR AUSTRALIA:	HOWARD BEALE
FOR BELGIUM:	OBERT DE THIEUSIES
FOR CHILE:	MARCIAL MORA
	E. GAJARDO
	JULIO ESCUDERO
FOR THE FRENCH REPUBLIC:	PIERRE CHARPENTIER
FOR JAPAN:	KOICHIRO ASAKAI
	T. SHIMODA
FOR NEW ZEALAND:	G. D. L. WHITE
FOR NORWAY:	PAUL KOHT
FOR THE UNION OF SOUTH AFRICA:	WENTZEL C. DU PLESSIS
FOR THE UNION OF SOVIET SOCIALIST REPUBLICS:	В. Кузнецов [1]
FOR THE UNITED KINGDOM OF GREAT BRITAIN AND NORTHERN IRELAND:	HAROLD CACCIA
FOR THE UNITED STATES OF AMERICA:	HERMAN PHLEGER
	PAUL C. DANIELS

---

[1] V. Kuznetsov.

Statements by the United States on the Occasion of the Signing of the Antarctic Treaty

Department of State press release 829, December 1

Statement by President Eisenhower [1]

I am gratified that The Antarctic Treaty is being signed today in Washington by the representatives of 12 nations. This Treaty is the result of the arduous and painstaking efforts of many people who for two years have worked to achieve this agreement of great importance to the world.

The Conference on Antarctica was convened October 15, 1959, as a result of a United States note of invitation, dated May 2, 1958, to those nations which had participated in scientific research in Antarctica during the 1957–1958 International Geophysical Year.

The spirit of cooperation and mutual understanding, which the 12 nations and their delegations exhibited in drafting a Treaty of this importance, should be an inspiring example of what can be accomplished by international cooperation in the field of science and in the pursuit of peace.

This Treaty guarantees that a large area of the world will be used only for peaceful purposes, assured by a system of inspection. Antarctica will constitute a laboratory for cooperative scientific research in accordance with treaty provisions. The legal status quo there will be maintained for the duration of the Treaty. Nuclear explosions are prohibited pending general international agreement on the subject.

The Antarctic Treaty and the guarantees it embodies constitute a significant advance toward the goal of a peaceful world with justice.

Department of State press release 831, December 1

Statement by Secretary of State Herter

The Governments of the United States of America, Argentina and Chile, on the occasion of the signing of the Antarctic Treaty, declare

---

[1] Read by Secretary of State Herter at the ceremony incidental to the signing of the Antarctic Treaty.

that the Antarctic Treaty does not affect their obligations under the Inter-American Treaty of Reciprocal Assistance, signed at Rio de Janeiro, Brazil, in 1947.[1]

Department of State press release 827, December 1

Statement Issued by the Department of State

The United States and 11 other nations signed The Antarctic Treaty in Washington today.

The Treaty, which was negotiated during the past 6 weeks, is based upon the principles that Antarctica will be used for peaceful purposes only and that the international scientific cooperation which characterized the 1957–1958 International Geophysical Year should continue.

The conference called to negotiate the treaty was convened at the initiative of the United States Government. On May 3, 1958, President Eisenhower announced that invitations had been extended to the Governments of the 11 nations which had carried on scientific research programs in Antarctica during the International Geophysical Year to participate in a conference with a view to writing a treaty "dedicated to the principle that the vast uninhabited wastes of Antarctica shall be used only for peaceful purposes." [2]

The following nations were invited: Argentina, Australia, Belgium, Chile, France, Japan, New Zealand, Norway, the Union of South Africa, the Union of Soviet Socialist Republics, and the United Kingdom.

At the treaty-signing ceremony today, Ambassador Herman Phleger, the U.S. Representative, and Ambassador Paul C. Daniels, Alternate U.S. Representative, signed for the United States.

The Treaty will not go into effect until it has been ratified by the 12 Governments. As regards the United States, this ratification would require the advice and consent of the Senate in accordance with constitutional processes. The instrument of ratification is issued by the President after a resolution of approval is agreed to by a two-thirds vote of the Senate.

The Treaty consists of a preamble and 14 articles. The Treaty provides that an area of the world as large as the United States and Europe together will be used for peaceful purposes only. An effective and unprecedented system of inspection on the Antarctic Continent is envisaged. Cooperative scientific research will be continued in the Antarctic region subject to the provisions of the Treaty. Until a gen-

---

[1] For text, see *Treaties and Other International Acts Series 1838* (62 Stat., pt. 2, p. 1681); also printed in *Department of State Bulletin*, Sept. 21, 1947, pp. 565–567.

[2] For the text of the invitation, see *ante*, pp. 2–4.

eral international agreement on nuclear explosions is reached, such explosions will be prohibited in Antarctica.

The Treaty is of indefinite duration, but after 30 years any party may call a conference for review and amendment. The Treaty provides that all territorial and sovereignty claims and the position of all the Governments regarding their recognition or non-recognition of such claims shall remain in status quo for the period of the Treaty. The Treaty is open to accession by other U.N. members and by such other states as may be agreed upon unanimously.

In order to further the purposes and the objectives of the Treaty a consultative committee will be established and will meet within 2 months of the entry into force of the Treaty and at suitable intervals thereafter to recommend measures to the participating parties. The first meeting will be at Canberra, Australia. In the meantime, the Conference recommended that representatives of the Governments meet at Washington at convenient times to discuss such arrangements as they might deem desirable.

The Conference on Antarctica convened in Washington October 15, 1959. At the first plenary session held that day, Ambassador Herman Phleger, the U.S. Representative, was named the Chairman of the Conference, and Henry E. Allen, the Secretary General. Ambassador Paul C. Daniels and George H. Owen were Alternate U.S. Representatives.

United States interest in Antarctica dates from the early part of the 19th century. One of the earliest achievements was the 1838–1842 expedition of Lieutenant Charles Wilkes which made sightings extending for 1,500 miles, thus proving the existence of the Antarctic Continent.

The period from 1928 to the present has been one of great activity. The names of Rear Admiral Richard E. Byrd, Lincoln Ellsworth, Captain Finn Ronne and Rear Admiral R. H. Cruzen [1] became intimately linked to Antarctica during this period. The U.S. Navy in 1946–47 organized the largest U.S. expedition to Antarctica. During the International Geophysical Year the United States established seven stations in Antarctica under the leadership of Rear Admiral George Dufek. At the present time four stations are being maintained, including one at the South Pole.

Scientific research in the Antarctic, coordinated and planned by the National Science Foundation, is made possible through the logistic support of the Navy Department with its long experience in polar operations. The U.S. Naval Support Force is commanded by Rear Admiral David N. Tyree.

---

[1] Leaders of U.S. expeditions to the Antarctic.

Report by the Secretary of State to the President on the Antarctic Treaty and the Final Act of the Conference, February 4, 1960

THE PRESIDENT:

I have the honor to submit to you, with a view to its transmission to the Senate for advice and consent to ratification, a certified copy of the Antarctic Treaty, signed at Washington on December 1, 1959 on behalf of the United States of America and eleven other countries. Those countries are Argentina, Australia, Belgium, Chile, the French Republic, Japan, New Zealand, Norway, the Union of South Africa, the Union of Soviet Socialist Republics, and the United Kingdom of Great Britain and Northern Ireland.

The treaty was formulated at the Conference on Antarctica held at Washington from October 15 to December 1, 1959. The idea for the conference was initiated by the Government of the United States which on May 2, 1958 extended an invitation to take part in such a conference to the eleven other countries which participated in the Antarctic program of the International Geophysical Year. A copy of the United States note of invitation, dated May 2, 1958, is enclosed for transmittal to the Senate for its information.[1]

Acceptances were received from all eleven Governments, and subsequently informal preparatory talks were held in Washington among representatives of the twelve countries. When the Conference convened on October 15, 1959 it used as a basis for discussion working papers considered in the course of the preparatory talks.

The treaty formulated at the Conference and signed on behalf of all twelve countries incorporates the basic purposes of the United States proposal and provides practical means for their fulfillment.

The treaty consists of a preamble and fourteen articles. It was drafted, as stated in the preamble, in recognition:

". . . that it is in the interest of all mankind that Antarctica shall continue forever to be used exclusively for peaceful purposes and shall not become the scene or object of international discord."

---

[1] For text, see *ante*, pp. 2–4.

The preamble also makes clear that the treaty is designed to further the purposes and principles embodied in the Charter of the United Nations.

Article I dedicates Antarctica to peaceful purposes only. It outlaws measures of a military nature, such as the establishment of military bases and fortifications, the carrying out of maneuvers, and the testing of weapons. It specifies that military personnel or equipment may be used there for scientific research or any other peaceful purpose. As the United States and a few other countries have conducted their Antarctic programs with logistic support provided by their military establishments, the latter provision was considered appropriate to dispel any doubt that peaceful programs could continue to be carried out in this way.

Article II provides that freedom of scientific investigation in Antarctica and cooperation toward that end, as applied during the International Geophysical Year, shall continue, subject to the provisions of the treaty.

Article III contains provisions for the promotion of such international scientific cooperation. Under its terms the Parties agree that scientists may be exchanged between expeditions and stations in Antarctica. The Parties also shall keep one another informed of their plans for scientific programs in Antarctica and shall make freely available scientific observations. Such exchanges would be made to the extent that the Parties consider it feasible and practicable. The Article also encourages the establishment of cooperative working relations with those Specialized Agencies of the United Nations and other international organizations having a scientific or technical interest in Antarctica.

Article IV specifies that nothing in the treaty will be interpreted as a renunciation of any Party's claim to sovereignty, as a renunciation or diminution of any Party's basis of claim, or as prejudicing the position of any Party regarding recognition or nonrecognition of another Party's claim or basis of claim. The Article also specifies that while the treaty is in force no acts or activities will constitute a basis for asserting, supporting or denying a claim or create any rights of sovereignty in Antarctica. It is finally provided that no new claims can be made and no existing claims enlarged while the treaty is in force.

It is believed that the manner in which the treaty deals with the sensitive problem of territorial claims is one of its most significant aspects. Seven of the twelve countries which signed the treaty have for many years asserted claims of sovereignty to portions of Antarctica, some of which overlap and have given rise to occasional frictions.

The claimants are Argentina, Australia, Chile, France, New Zealand, Norway, and the United Kingdom. Neither the United States nor the Soviet Union has made any territorial claims, nor do they recognize the claims of others. Other nonclaimant countries which are signatories to the treaty are Belgium, Japan, and the Union of South Africa. In essence, Article IV minimizes the possibility that disputes over claims to sovereignty will erupt and interfere with constructive scientific work in Antarctica.

Article V bans all nuclear explosions in Antarctica and the dumping there of radioactive waste material pending the conclusion of international agreements on nuclear uses. In effect this provision prevents Antarctica from being used as a nuclear proving ground or as a dumping ground for radioactive wastes. It prevents the possibility that harmful fallout will be carried to neighboring regions. However, this article does not prevent the use of nuclear energy in atomic power plants.

Article VI establishes the zone of application of the treaty. By its terms the treaty applies to the area south of 60° South Latitude, including ice shelves, that is, thick portions of ice attached to the land and extending seaward; but the rights of any State under international law with regard to the high seas within the area are not affected.

Article VII contains provisions designed to ensure that the peaceful intent of the treaty is being carried out. It permits the signatory Parties, and any acceding Parties qualified to participate in the consultative meetings, to send observers anywhere in Antarctica at any time. The observers must be nationals of the sending Party and their designation must be made known to every other Party having the right to send observers. They are to have complete freedom of access to all areas of Antarctica and must be permitted to inspect stations, installations, and equipment as well as ships and aircraft at points of discharging or embarking cargoes or personnel in Antarctica. Aerial observation by any country having the right to send observers is also permitted. Parties are required to furnish advance notice of all Antarctic expeditions by their ships or nationals and all Antarctic expeditions organized in or proceeding from their territories. They must also report all stations in Antarctica occupied by their nationals and all military personnel or equipment intended to be sent to Antarctica for peaceful purposes. The requirement to give advance information would not, of course, prevent previously notified plans from being modified or revised, upon further notice, whenever advisable because of unforeseen events such as budgetary limitations, weather, or damages to ships or equipment.

Under Article VIII each Party has exclusive jurisdiction over its own nationals who are observers designated under the treaty for inspection purposes or scientific personnel exchanged between expeditions or stations in Antarctica, in respect of all acts or omissions, occurring while such persons are in Antarctica for the purpose of exercising their functions. Members of the staffs accompanying such persons are also covered. The positions of the Parties relating to jurisdiction over all other persons in Antarctica are not affected. The Parties agree to consult together immediately should any dispute arise concerning the exercise of jurisdiction in Antarctica.

Under Article IX, representatives of the twelve signatory States are to meet in Canberra, Australia within two months after the treaty enters into force and thereafter at times and places which they deem suitable. Their functions will be to exchange information, to consult together on matters of common interest pertaining to Antarctica, and to recommend to their Governments measures in furtherance of the principles and objectives of the treaty. These measures are to become effective when approved by all of the Parties who were entitled to participate in the meetings held to consider those measures.

A country which has become party to the treaty by accession may qualify to participate in the meetings during such time as it demonstrates its interest in Antarctica by conducting substantial scientific research there.

Representatives participating in the meetings will receive the reports of observers carrying out inspection under the treaty.

Regardless of whether measures to facilitate the exercise of treaty rights are adopted, all rights established by the treaty, including, of course, rights to conduct inspection, may be exercised from the date the treaty enters into force.

By Article X the Parties are obliged to exert appropriate efforts, consistent with the Charter of the United Nations, to see that no one engages in any activity in Antarctica contrary to the principles of the treaty. Its aim is not only to prevent such activity by nationals and organizations under the jurisdiction of the Parties but to deter countries which are not parties to the treaty and their nationals and organizations, from engaging in nonpeaceful activities in Antarctica. In effect it pledges the Parties not only to refrain from giving assistance to persons or countries which might engage in nonpeaceful activities or atomic tests in Antarctica, but to take active steps to discourage any such activity.

Under Article XI disputes among the Parties arising under the treaty are to be resolved by peaceful means of their own choice, such as arbitration, conciliation, or the like. If this proves unsuccessful, the dispute is to be referred to the International Court of Justice, with the consent of all parties to the dispute.

Article XII provides a method for modifying or amending the treaty at any time by unanimous consent of the Parties entitled to participate in the consultative meetings. An amendment will enter into force when all such Parties give notice that they have ratified it. Parties not entitled to participate in the meetings may accept the amendment within two years. If they fail to do so within that time they will be deemed to have withdrawn from the treaty.

The treaty has no specified duration, but Article XII provides that after thirty years any of the Parties participating in consultative meetings may ask for a conference to review the operation of the treaty. Amendments approved at such a conference by a majority of those represented, including a majority of the consultative Parties, will enter into force when ratified by all of the consultative Parties. If a modification or amendment approved at such a conference does not enter into force within two years, any country may withdraw from the treaty, effective two years from its notification to that effect.

Article XIII provides that the treaty will enter into force when ratified by all twelve signatory States. It contains an accession clause by which countries other than the original twelve may acquire the rights and assume the obligations embodied in the treaty. All States Members of the United Nations and any other State which is unanimously invited by the consultative Parties may accede.

Article XIII also names the United States as depositary Government and contains other provisions of a formal nature relating to ratification, accession, and registration with the United Nations.

By Article XIV the English, French, Russian, and Spanish language versions of the treaty are declared to be equally authentic.

On the occasion of the signing of the Antarctic Treaty the Governments of the United States, Argentina, and Chile declared[1] that the treaty does not affect their obligations under the Inter-American Treaty of Reciprocal Assistance, signed at Rio de Janeiro on September 2, 1947 (62 Stat. 1681).

The United States Representative to the Conference on Antarctica was Ambassador Herman Phleger, former Legal Adviser of the Department of State. Alternate Representatives were Ambassador Paul C. Daniels and Mr. George H. Owen. The United States Delegation included, in addition to officers of the Department of State, a representative of the Department of Defense. Congressional advisers were the Honorable Frank Carlson and the Honorable Gale W. McGee, United States Senators. The Delegation received advice directly from the National Science Foundation, the agency responsible for coordinating the planning and management of the United

---

[1] See *ante*, pp. 68–69.

States scientific program in Antarctica. It was also advised by a committee of six distinguished scientists appointed by the National Academy of Sciences because of their active interest in scientific investigations in Antarctica.[1]

There is transmitted for your information, and for that of the Senate, the Final Act of the Conference on Antarctica, signed at Washington on December 1, 1959 by plenipotentiaries of the twelve participating nations.[2] The Final Act does not require ratification.

I believe that the signing of the Antarctic Treaty is a substantial achievement. Its ratification by all of the signatory States would further, in an entire continent, peaceful cooperation in the attainment of scientific progress. It is based on the will to maintain peace in an important area of the world. The United States, which has engaged in extensive exploratory and scientific activities in Antarctica, initiated the idea of the Antarctic Treaty, which is believed to be in the best interests of this country and of all mankind. It is hoped therefore that the United States may be among the first to ratify it.

Respectfully submitted,

CHRISTIAN A. HERTER

THE PRESIDENT,
   The White House.

---

[1] For additional information regarding this advisory committee, see *Department of State Bulletin*, Nov. 2, 1959, p. 651.

[2] For text, see *ante*, pp. 56–60.

Message by the President to the Senate Transmitting the Antarctic Treaty And the Final Act of the Conference, February 15, 1960

To the Senate of the United States:

With a view to receiving the advice and consent of the Senate to ratification, I transmit herewith a certified copy of the Antarctic Treaty, signed at Washington on December 1, 1959, by plenipotentiaries of the United States of America and eleven other countries.

This is a unique and historic treaty. It provides that a large area of the world—an area equal in size to Europe and the United States combined—will be used for peaceful purposes only. It contains a broad, unrestricted inspection system to ensure that the nonmilitarization provisions will be carried out.

The purposes and provisions of the treaty are explained in the report of the Secretary of State which is transmitted herewith.

I transmit also, for the information of the Senate, a certified copy of the Final Act of the Conference on Antarctica, held at Washington October 15 to December 1, 1959, at which the treaty was formulated. The Final Act does not require ratification.

I am gratified to recall that it was at the initiative of the United States that the Conference on Antarctica was convened. On May 2, 1958 the United States extended to the eleven other countries which participated in the Antarctic program of the International Geophysical Year an invitation to participate in a conference to consider the conclusion of a treaty on Antarctica for certain stated purposes. The invitation was accepted by all eleven countries: Argentina, Australia, Belgium, Chile, the French Republic, Japan, New Zealand, Norway, the Union of South Africa, the Union of Soviet Socialist Republics, and the United Kingdom of Great Britain and Northern Ireland.

The spirit of cooperation and mutual understanding with which representatives of the twelve countries drafted the Antarctic Treaty and signed it for their respective Governments is an inspiring example of what can be accomplished by international cooperation in the field of science and in the pursuit of peace.

I believe that the Antarctic Treaty is a significant advance toward the goal of a peaceful world with justice. In the hope that the United States, which initiated the idea of the Antarctic Treaty, may be one of the first to ratify it, I recommend that the Senate give it early and favorable consideration.

DWIGHT D. EISENHOWER

CPSIA information can be obtained at www.ICGtesting.com
Printed in the USA
LVOW011918310513

336418LV00013B/443/P

9 781258 642105